HAPPY PARENT, HAPPY CHILD

A 10-step plan for a stress-free family life

Dr Genevieve von Lob

CORGI BOOKS

TRANSWORLD PUBLISHERS
61–63 Uxbridge Road, London W5 5SA
www.penguin.co.uk

Transworld is part of the Penguin Random House group of companies
whose addresses can be found at global.penguinrandomhouse.com

Penguin
Random House
UK

First published in Great Britain in 2017 as *Five Deep Breaths* by Bantam Press
an imprint of Transworld Publishers
Corgi edition published as *Happy Parent, Happy Child* 2018

Every effort has been made to obtain the necessary permissions with
reference to copyright material, both illustrative and quoted. We apologize for
any omissions in this respect and will be pleased to make the
appropriate acknowledgements in any future edition.

A CIP catalogue record for this book
is available from the British Library.

ISBN
9780552176002

Typeset in 10.75/15.5pt Palatino LT Pro by Jouve (UK), Milton Keynes.
Printed and bound in Great Britain by Clays Ltd, Elcograf S.p.A.

Penguin Random House is committed to a sustainable
future for our business, our readers and our planet. This book
is made from Forest Stewardship Council® certified paper.

MIX
Paper from
responsible sources
FSC® C018179

1 3 5 7 9 10 8 6 4 2

HAPPY PARENT, HAPPY CHILD

To all parents: past, present and future

Contents

Before we begin

Welcome to *Happy Parent, Happy Child*. I wrote this book to share the work I do with families with a wider audience, and I hope you will find it a valuable and inspiring companion on your journey as a parent.

For the sake of simplicity, I have tended to refer to parents as 'mums and dads' – though the word 'parent' can of course mean different things to different people. For some, a parent could be a grandparent, aunt, uncle, friend or stepparent, adoptive parent, foster carer or guardian. Some parents are in same-sex or transgender couples, and all come from different ethnic, religious and cultural backgrounds. Throughout *Happy Parent, Happy Child*, the term 'parent' is intended to include all this diversity.

I am a chartered member of the British Psychological Society and the Health and Care Professions Council, and abide by their codes of ethics. I have not used any confidential material from my therapeutic work with clients in this book. All the 'case studies' featured in these pages are made-up composites designed to illustrate different themes I encounter in my work. All names are fictional, and any resemblance to real people is purely coincidental.

BEFORE WE BEGIN

I have also drawn on extensive interviews with parents who kindly agreed to discuss their experiences with me for the purposes of my research and gave me their consent to use the material anonymously in this book. Where reported speech appears in quote marks, it should be read as a paraphrasing to illustrate a general point, rather than a direct quotation.

Happy Parent, Happy Child is not a substitute for professional support. I have included a list of helpful resources including organizations, websites and books on specific topics (page 261). Although I discuss mental health problems including anxiety, panic attacks, depression, ADHD and others, a detailed exploration of these and other medical conditions is beyond the scope of this book.

Some of the exercises I describe could potentially cause you to experience strong emotions. If at any time you feel you need more support, I would recommend you seek professional advice. Above all, I hope *Happy Parent, Happy Child* will be a source of encouragement and reassurance that will endure long after you've turned the final page.

Dr Genevieve von Lob
London, June 2018
www.drvonlob.com / @drvonLob

Ripping up the rule book

On the face of it, I might seem like the world's least qualified person to write a book for new mums and dads. I only became a parent myself eight months ago, when my daughter Matilda was born, and I grew up in a less than conventional family setting. I'd therefore like to take a moment to explain how I became a clinical psychologist working with hundreds of parents, teenagers and children from every conceivable type of background. Having spent years in both private practice and front-line NHS and local government mental health services, I've had the privilege of helping many mums and dads find their own answers to the dilemmas of modern parenting. Every day I'm awed and inspired by the courage and creativity of the parents and young people I meet, and I wrote this book to share something of the lessons we've learned together along the way.

My mother, Amanda, was a seventies wild child who in her late teens moved into a hippy commune in Norwich, where she scraped by singing in pubs and clubs. By the time I was born, she had grown into a headstrong twenty-two-year-old and I suspect my arrival was not entirely planned – I never knew the identity of my biological father. My mother later told me that having me spurred her to seek a clearer direction and on a whim she started singing lessons. To everyone's amazement, she beat intense competition to win a scholarship to train as an opera singer at the Royal Academy of Music in London. Determined to fulfil her ambition of becoming an international mezzo-soprano, she bundled me up along with a suitcase and moved us to a council flat in a tower block in Stepney Green. I had just turned two.

Though I could always sense my mother's love, our life together was a confusing juxtaposition of the grind of surviving in an almost penniless single-parent household on an East End estate and the glamorous world of opera, where I served as her shy sidekick – to the amusement, delight and sometimes consternation of her colleagues. Constantly dashing between rehearsals and classes, she would plonk me backstage, where a flamboyant cast of actors, singers and musicians arrayed in ball gowns or period costume would extravagantly fuss over me – an incongruous presence in the decidedly adult world of Mozart and Verdi. To my child's eyes, the immaculately made-up women looked like angels. Tiring of the attention, I would embark on lone expeditions deep into the hallowed corridors of the Academy – charting my path via the trill of a piano scale or the flourish of a clarinet. I dreaded returning to our tiny flat, where my mother was forced to accept a procession of lodgers to pay the bills. These strangers – as a child I called them 'the creatures' – would turn up unannounced, doss down on the sofa and help themselves to the meagre contents of our fridge.

My mother loved to share her beautiful voice and would warble scales as she did the housework. Her soaring mezzo tones were so powerful that I once saw her break a glass – causing her to collapse into giggles. But even her joyful octaves could not lift the oppressive atmosphere of the estate. I would regularly miss meals because she would run out of money, or she would be stuck at rehearsals as I was passed around among neighbours, and I was jealous of my mother's boyfriends, who often behaved as if I didn't exist. I can vividly remember the wash of relief I felt when, at the age of four, it was decided that I would temporarily return to Norwich to live with my grandparents while my mother completed her studies.

Despite our tough start, my mother's opera career began to blossom. She started doing television and theatre work and planned to set up her own travelling opera company so we could live together in Norwich. She put down a deposit on a beautiful Victorian house and took me to see my future bedroom – a wonderful converted attic. I couldn't wait to move in. The next morning, I was watching children's television when my grandparents did something unusual: they turned off the set and sat down with me on the sofa. They told me that my mother had been killed in a car accident while driving home to London the previous night. I was nine. My relatives were consumed by such grief that they found it impossible to talk to me about my feelings because they were struggling so hard to contain their own. I poured my pent-up emotion into an obsessive devotion to music, spending almost every spare minute of my childhood and teenage years learning to play the piano, dance, act and sing.

The next turning point came during my first year at university. I had been offered a place at a prestigious drama school, but my grandparents could not afford the fees and so I began a psychology degree instead – though I still harboured secret dreams of following in my mother's footsteps as a professional performer. One sweltering afternoon in exam season I was opening an antiquated sash window in the halls of residence when I slipped and fell. The glass shattered and I was rushed to hospital gushing blood from a deep gash in my right palm. My first thought was that I may never again play the piano.

While the injury was bad enough, the most painful part of the experience was the way the over-stretched medical staff seemed to look at me as dispassionately as if I were a specimen on a slab. It was only months later, when a physiotherapist showed a genuine curiosity about how I was feeling, that I felt anybody really cared. She spoke to me with such kindness that I broke down. Though our months of work together would save my hand from curling into a permanent claw, I was equally grateful for the interest she showed in my inner world. I realized that my future lay not in the performing arts, but in learning to extend to others the listening ear the physiotherapist had offered me. I embarked on the decade-long path of study needed to become a doctor of clinical psychology.

The doctoral training was unlike any other educational experience I had encountered. Our instructors encouraged us to work with our own childhood wounds to try to understand our present-day conflicts and troubling emotions. It was only by doing this work on ourselves that we could hope to be of use to anybody else. During the course, two more major life events occurred. When I was twenty-six, I lost my cousin Graeme – who was like a brother to me – to leukaemia. The following year I discovered the body of a flatmate – one of my best friends – who had died in the bath. Coupled with my losses in childhood, these experiences left me with a profound sense of unresolved grief – but they also served as a spur to the interior work that would later help me to reach others trapped in their own dark tunnels.

Throughout my journey, and my subsequent work with clients – from angry East End teenagers to stressed-out City executives – I have learned the value of exploring unwanted feelings. So often our dark moods or fears can seem like enemies; they can leave us feeling isolated and alone. But life has taught me that there is a way to work with these emotions and find the peace that lies just beyond them – if we can muster the courage and curiosity to keep going forward.

How my 10-step plan can help you

When it comes to raising children, there's no shortage of advice on offer. Friends, family, magazines, books and blogs – all are brimming with opinions on how to give your child the best chance of growing up happy, bright and successful. With so many options available, and so many contradictory theories, it's easy to start questioning whether you are making the right choices, or even secretly to wish there was some fail-safe manual on how to be a parent.

Happy Parent, Happy Child is not that manual, because such a manual could never exist. Every child is unique, and the society they are growing up in is changing so fast that what may have worked yesterday might not be so relevant today. Some parents tell me they could never have imagined the weight of responsibility they would feel for somebody else's well-being until they experienced the joy of becoming parents themselves. It's all very well for experts to say that it's good for a child to undergo a few knocks and setbacks from time to time – but in reality, what parent wants to see their child suffer, even for a moment?

As parents, we can learn to become more comfortable with the fact that much of the time we're just doing our best to muddle through, and that's okay. Parenting inevitably involves periods of worry or doubt, and for anybody navigating choppier waters, I hope *Happy Parent, Happy Child* will be both a reassuring companion and a source of practical guidance on how to tune in to your intuition and deepen your connection with your child.

In parenting, there is no such thing as getting it 'right'. There's not a human being in history who has had the perfect upbringing, and any attempt to be a perfect parent is doomed to fail. There is no one-size-fits-all formula: everybody's experience as a mum or dad is different, and nobody will ever fully understand the unique set of challenges another person faces. Even within a family, siblings can have completely contrasting personalities and relate to their parents in different ways, while raising a child who has a disability or long-term illness can present its own set of dilemmas. Nevertheless, having helped many parents from a wide range of backgrounds to experience a greater sense of confidence, ease and flow, I wrote *Happy Parent, Happy Child* to offer the essence of my one-on-one work to a broader audience.

In the following pages, I want to help parents move from the kinds of feelings shown below on the left to those on the right:

I don't know if I'm doing the right thing.	*I'm handling myself better as a parent.*
I feel overwhelmed and I can't think straight.	*I'm more confident and I'm being kinder to myself.*
I'm not sure if I'm a good enough role model.	*I feel a greater sense of connection with my child.*
It's all my fault.	*I'm better at managing my children's moods – and my own.*
I'm always being judged.	*I'm learning to trust myself.*

A better relationship with your child

The quality of the relationship we have with our kids needs to be at the core of every parenting journey. I like to summarize the key components of this kind of connection with the acronym HEART ♥:

- **H**umility. A willingness to accept that we are not perfect, but we simply do the best we can in the moment while aspiring to live by our values.

- **E**mpathy. Empathize with your child by remembering to take a moment to try to see the world through their eyes. Recognize that they have legitimate concerns and views.

- **A**uthenticity. In our busy lives as parents, stress can easily take over. The daily grind leaves us little space to explore how we truly feel. Authenticity is about having the courage to look at what's really going on for us.

- **R**espect. Respect is a two-way street, so respect yourself as an experienced adult whose well-being is just as important as that of your child. And respect your child by acknowledging that, while you may know more, they too have valuable lessons to teach.

- **T**rust. Trust yourself and your child, and believe that you can both handle life's ups and downs. Give them a chance to make mistakes in a safe, contained way that allows them to learn and grow.

Of course, all this can sound wonderful in theory, but the messy reality of modern parenting is rarely quite so simple. Nevertheless, children will have a much better chance of thriving if parents have access to tools that can help them provide the kind of calm and confident leadership they need. The rest of this book is about finding ways to embody these HEART-centred values – first in your relationship with yourself, and then with your child.

Dilemmas of the modern parent

Happy Parent, Happy Child is not going to tell you what kind of parent you should be. My aim is to encourage and support you to look within – to be your own guru and listen to your own guidance. In my work, I'm struck by how many parents find it difficult to trust themselves. No matter what background they may have, or what particular issue they are facing, the core of the problem often consists of a lack of self-worth or a feeling of not being good enough. These are not the kinds of feelings we tend to discuss, but they have reached enormous proportions in our society. So before we even begin to start work in my sessions, I find it often helps to share a broader perspective on the challenges of modern parenting to prove to worried mums and dads that they are far from alone.

We belong to a unique generation. We tend to be more open about our feelings than our parents or certainly our grandparents, and more aware of the influence our own upbringing may have had on the way we relate to our children. This greater level of self-awareness means that parents these days are often more willing to admit that they feel they're not getting it 'right' or that they're struggling with problems, such as anxiety or post-natal depression. Whether they reach out to friends or therapists, or share what they're going through online, parents are more open and more prepared to express their concerns than ever before. Blogs documenting the many difficulties of raising kids have reinforced this new culture of honesty around parenting and provided a valuable sense of solidarity for many mums and dads.

This greater self-awareness is a wonderful blessing in terms of helping us to understand ourselves and others. But it can also foster a gnawing fear that our children will fail to fulfil their potential or even resent us when they're older if we fail to conform to our model of an 'ideal' parent. Or we may start over-analysing – worrying that we might somehow be projecting an unaddressed conflict within ourselves on to our child. While the ease with which we can now read about the everyday struggles fellow parents are facing might be comforting, it can also feed niggling doubts about whether we're doing enough for our own children. In today's technology-driven and consumerist society, there seem to be so many choices to make. Which school? What should they be eating? How much time on the screen? What about social media? How about time for outdoor play and connecting with nature? What activities should they be doing? Are we setting the right limits? Are we spending enough time with them?

Answering these questions is hard enough, but in our hyper-connected online world it's easy to feel that we're constantly being judged. We are addicted to comparing ourselves with others – and it's so easy to do as it's only a click away. Here are some of the themes that often surface in my conversations with parents:

- **Parenting as a competition.** It's natural for parents to want to do a good job, but many are telling me they feel as if they have been unwillingly thrust into an unspoken competition. Mums and dads often experience intense pressure to provide the same toys, phones, computers, activities or holidays as other parents because they don't want their own children to feel left out. Parents can also find themselves competing intensely to get their child into the 'right' school. It's very easy to think you're failing or not giving your kids enough opportunities, even though we all know deep down that forming a strong emotional connection with our child is more important in the long run than anything money can buy.

- **Feeling judged.** Working mums and dads can find themselves silently at odds with those who have given up their jobs to become full-time parents, injecting the same level of professionalism into making fancy-dress costumes or cupcakes as they did into their careers. Full-time mums or dads may, in turn, mourn the loss of their work status and feel that their partners undervalue the contribution they make. They may even feel resentful about dedicating these years entirely to raising a family.

- **Pressure-cooker classrooms.** Academic demands on children are constantly growing. One fourteen-year-old girl told me she was struggling to sleep at night because she was so anxious about the pressure placed on her by teachers – themselves under pressure to meet targets. Another anxious teen told me she was convinced she would end up homeless if she did not pass with flying colours. One child who was refusing to do his homework told me he'd been at school all day and needed a better 'work–life' balance – and he was only eight. Everyone wants their child to do well, but many parents are concerned that their children are being put under too much pressure by a 'factory-farm' school system where assessments are being conducted at ever younger ages. Academic research has shown that play is essential for healthy brain development, but recreation is increasingly being squeezed out of timetables.

- **Time famine.** For many parents, balancing the competing demands of the workplace, parenthood and perhaps caring for their own older parents can seem like an impossible task. Days can turn into a struggle just to keep your head above water and you may feel constantly stretched to the limit.

● **Sleep deprivation.** Sleep deprivation is a form of torture, and everything is harder when you're tired. So many parents tell me they feel like they're running on empty so much of the time that they feel constantly on edge.

● **Criticism – from self and others.** Sometimes our parents, friends or relatives may offer well-intentioned advice, but usually our harshest judge is ourself. All of us have inherited a template – perhaps without realizing it – of what an 'ideal' family should look like. We may find ourselves struggling to live up to impossible goals, or driven to over-compensate for what we perceive as our own parents' failings. Or we may fear that people will interpret our attempts to set appropriate limits as a sign of emotional coldness or a controlling personality, and that they will perhaps conclude that we don't really love our child.

● **Digital dilemmas.** Social media is magnifying peer pressure – for children and their parents. Young girls pout for selfies, teenagers constantly compare their looks with those of their peers or media stars, and old-fashioned bullying has migrated into cyberspace. Many mums and dads are also concerned about what kind of images their children may be exposed to online, what they're reading and who they may be communicating with. Parents feel the pressure too – bombarded by endless pictures posted by other mums or dads, or stories of celebrities who seem to have the perfect family, the perfect marriage, the perfect body and the perfect life.

● **Building resilience.** We all know that children need opportunities to learn that it's okay to make mistakes or experience failure. Only by working through challenges and overcoming setbacks can they develop the resilience they will need to navigate the inevitable ups and downs of adult life. But it can be hard to strike a balance between letting your child explore and take risks and the discomfort you may feel when they struggle. How do we know what's right?

● **A drought of self-compassion.** In our society, we're all much too hard on ourselves. We're brought up to believe that 'success' is all-important, whether it's at school, in our jobs, in our relationships and especially as parents. We can spend a great deal of energy pushing ourselves – and then beating ourselves up when things don't work out as planned. This harsh attitude can easily spill over into our attempts to be a little calmer. Many of us hold ourselves to impossible standards as parents and find it very difficult to accept that being 'good enough' is okay.

The stakes have never been higher – not just for parents, but for society as a whole. There can be no more important task than providing a firm foundation for the next generation to grow into independent, well-balanced and resourceful adults brimming with inspiration for building a better world. Yet with all these dilemmas to face, and all the conflicting advice, it's easy to feel that as a parent, you just can't win. This book will help you get back in control.

The five key points

Ripping up the rule book

- Today's parents face unique challenges: you're not alone.

- There's no rule book for parenting: learn to trust yourself.

- The quality of the parent–child forms the core of every parenting journey.

- A HEART-centred connection will last a lifetime.

- There is no more important task than bringing up the next generation.

Sort yourself out first

It's 6:23 a.m. You've just managed to roll out of bed and stumble bleary-eyed into the kitchen in search of a coffee, only to find your six-year-old bouncing with energy and determined to play. She has her own ideas about what an enjoyable start to the day looks like – and it doesn't involve getting dressed for school. She's much more interested in rebuilding the den she made out of cushions in the living room last night. Meanwhile, your eight-year-old is in his room, slumped into his pillows and no doubt already immersed in Minecraft on the iPad, while your thirteen-year-old still hasn't woken up. You have only one goal: to get all three dressed and fed and out the door with a fighting chance of making it to school on time, preferably with their teeth brushed and their shoes laced. 'Muuuum,' your six-year-old says, suddenly bored of her den-reconstruction project. 'I know you won't say "yes" – but can I watch TV?'

It's only the hundredth time you've had this conversation – and the outcome will depend purely on how exhausted you're feeling. In this case, you decide to put your foot down. Your six-year-old scrunches up her face and says, 'I don't even *like* you,' before storming off to her room, where you can be pretty certain she won't be getting ready. By this point, your thirteen-year-old has dragged himself out of bed and is asking if you've got his gym kit ready and found his missing homework. As you serve breakfast, all three siblings start arguing with each other. Your six-year-old spills her juice, runs away from the table and starts chasing the dog.

An edge creeps into your voice as you tell her as calmly as possible to get her shoes on, but she looks you straight in the eye, then turns and runs away again. Before you can help it, you've lost your temper and you're screaming at all three of them, 'We've got ten minutes. Can we please all just get a *move on*!'

When we go from calm to losing it

Most parents I work with can relate to some aspect of this situation. Perhaps you feel exasperated when you are forced to repeat yourself over and over again with kids who don't seem to listen? Maybe you're able to remain patient and calm for much of the day, but by evening, you're so tired that you start snapping. So many parents end up losing their temper and feeling guilty about it afterwards. Let's talk about how we can stay calm.

Change starts with you

During the safety briefing on every plane journey, adults are reminded that they should secure their own oxygen masks in an emergency before they help their children fit theirs. Why? Because it helps them to look after their children more effectively. The same is true of our emotional well-being. We won't be able to support our kids to stay calm and balanced if we are out of control ourselves.

Children are like tuning forks: they will pick up on what the adults around them are going through, even if these adults are doing their best to keep their true feelings hidden. You can't expect your kids to stop having tantrums if you are resorting to yelling and falling apart yourself. This is something every parent knows deep down, but sometimes it can feel an impossible ask. So *how* do we stay cool when the pressure is on?

Understand how stress affects your body

The first step towards mastering stress is to notice how it feels in your body. Let's try it now. Take a few moments to imagine a stressful parenting situation as vividly as you can, as if it is happening to you right now. What thoughts are going through your head? What sensations do you feel in your body?

When you slow down to notice what's going on for you physically, you may notice that stress causes physical sensations, such as tension in your stomach or tightness in your chest. By learning to recognize when the stress of daily life has triggered a response in our body, we can take a moment to slow down, check in with ourselves and step out of these automatic survival responses. We remember to pause, take a deep breath and choose how we want to respond to a situation, rather than react.

The Fight-Flight-Freeze response

It helps if we know a bit about what's going on in our brains when we feel stressed. In the centre of our brain is a small almond-shaped organ called the amygdala. The amygdala is like the brain's 'smoke alarm' – it switches on when we think we are in danger. When our ancestors encountered a rampaging woolly mammoth, the amygdala would send a message to the body to start pumping out stress hormones such as cortisol and adrenaline in preparation for one of three things:

- **Flight.** We feel a rush of fear, and the body gears up to escape.

- **Fight.** We feel a flash of anger, and the body prepares to attack.

- **Freeze.** We are frozen to the spot in terror.

We may not face life-threatening situations very often these days, but our brain's fight-flight-or-freeze response can still be triggered many times each day. Our modern-day equivalents of woolly mammoths can be anything from our children squabbling to a stressful parents' evening or feeling judged by our mother-in-law. Think of the jolt of fear we feel when our child doesn't return home on time, or the surge of anger we experience at being cut up in traffic on the school run.

In these cases, the primitive, emotional part of our brain takes over and we can't think straight because the logical part of the brain has gone offline.

Remembering to breathe

We can't think clearly when we are feeling stressed. The first thing we need to do is calm down the stress response in our system. Breathing more slowly and deeply is the simplest and quickest way we can do that.

Picture a car speeding down a motorway at 100 m.p.h.: that's the build-up of stress. Taking slow, deep breaths engages something called the Vagus nerve, which acts like a brake. This huge nerve connects our brain with our heart and other major organs before meandering all the way down into the depths of our gut. (The word *vagus* in Latin means 'wandering' – the word 'vagabond' has the same root.)

When we breathe deeply, the Vagus nerve has a soothing effect: our heart rate slows, our blood pressure falls and we reduce production of the stress hormone cortisol. We also strengthen the pathways in the brain associated with a sense of calm. The next time you feel stressed, take five deep breaths and feel your entire body soften and your frazzled feelings start to fade. (Recent studies have shown that the Vagus nerve also responds to human connection and physical touch, so a hug works too.)

Try It: Use your breath to calm down

Notice how you are breathing. Bringing your attention to your breath for even ten seconds has a noticeably calming effect on the body. Is it shallow or deep? Are you holding your breath, tightening your stomach or hunching your shoulders?

● Inhale deeply through the nose for a count of five, making sure that the tummy expands. It can help to imagine it filling up with air like a balloon. There's no need to strain. If it feels unnatural to breathe into the belly, then simply breathe as deeply as you can into your chest.

● Hold the breath for a count of five. If the mind wanders, gently come back to the breath – without judging yourself for losing focus.

- Then exhale completely through the mouth. Really feel like you're letting it all go. The out-breath should take a little longer than the in-breath.

- It can be helpful to place your hands on your tummy so that you can really feel the expansion and contraction as you breathe in and out.

Repeat this several times until you are feeling a little more relaxed.

Breathe more deeply, live more deeply

The beauty of this practice is that it's easy to make it part of your daily life – it's simply a question of bringing more attention to what you are already doing all the time. I find many parents benefit from building little reminders into their day to take five deep breaths until it becomes a habit. For example:

- A bedside reminder to start the day with five deep breaths.

- Take a breath every time you find yourself waiting for the kids in the morning/before serving dinner/ before putting them to bed.

- Taking slow breaths until a red traffic light changes to green.

- When you're waiting for the kettle to boil.

- Before you reply to a text message or email.

- There are also apps that you can program to remind you to breathe (see page 282 for some suggestions).

There's no great mystery to this exercise – it's just a way of tapping in to our in-built relaxation system. Change doesn't happen overnight, but as you familiarize yourself with your breath, you will discover an anchor-line that you can always use to return to the present, no matter how much your mind wants to rake over the past or worry about what might happen in the future. By learning to breathe more deeply, we learn to live more deeply in the only place and time there is: the here and now.

Remember: it's normal to find parenting a struggle

I have worked with hundreds of families and I can assure you that every single mum and dad has times when they feel like a terrible parent. All of us have moments when we want to run away from it all, or long to spend an evening on our own with a hot bath followed by a good night's sleep. Far from feeling filled with love for our children, we might feel like parenting is just a never-ending list of chores. It's normal to have times – maybe many times – when you just don't enjoy parenting very much. Remembering that this is how many other parents are feeling can help us get through the day.

Have realistic expectations of yourself

Dealing with a child who won't do what they are told is really tough at the end of a long day. Be realistic about how much you can deal with without getting stressed. Sometimes we can't help losing our tempers. Rather than beating ourselves up for being human, we would do better to accept where we are right now: stressed-out, sleep deprived and miserable. We can accept that we won't always create a peaceful and harmonious home because nobody can. No parent is perfect. Everyone has their bad days. And every new day is a chance to try again.

Use painful feelings as fuel for change

When we feel we've made mistakes in our parenting, it's easy to start feeling sorry for ourselves or start thinking we are victims. That doesn't help you or your kids. We all experience times when we realize we could have done things differently. Go easy on yourself, think about how you would approach a similar situation in the future, and remember we're all learning as we go along.

Avoid the comparison trap

Comparing ourselves with others will bring us down. We can all look at other mums and dads who seem to have a bigger house, keep on top of chores effortlessly, and serve their children homemade organic meals every night. So what? We are all on unique journeys as parents. Every family is different. What really matters is that you are doing what you can to be the kind of parent you want to be. What others appear to be doing is irrelevant.

Sleep is necessary – know your limits

We all know that parenting – especially when it comes to babies and younger kids – can lead to a chronic lack of sleep. Don't make it any harder for yourself than is necessary. Sometimes it's okay to go to bed really early and get under the duvet. Get more rest and try again tomorrow.

Ask for help

Communicate clearly to your partner, wider family and friends what practical steps they can take to help you. So many assume that those close to us should know what we need without us even having to ask. But you'll be doing the people you care about – and your kids – a big favour if you spell out clearly how they can help, especially if you're going through a tough time.

Julie: Remembering to breathe

'I'm really noticing a difference if I can just remember to take a deep breath a bit more often, and not always be thinking about everything I have to do. I know when Ben comes in from school I've got a million things on my mind – I'm doing the cooking but I'm thinking about when I'm going to get a chance to take the cat to the vet. I go through the motions of asking Ben how his day went – but I miss half of what he's actually saying because my mind's racing ahead. I'll ask him about how his Maths test went over dinner and he'll look all crestfallen and say, "I already told you earlier."

'By focusing on one thing at a time, I'm getting better at noticing when I'm getting distracted. I try not to get annoyed with myself and try to take a few more deep breaths to keep myself anchored in the present. When Ben comes in I try to focus more on him and what he's saying. I've found that even thirty seconds of being fully there with him is much better than just saying, "That's nice, love," and carrying on with other things. It doesn't matter if I don't have time for a long chat – we can always pick up on things later – but just those few moments of real connection make a big difference to us both.'

The five key points

Sort yourself out first

- Change starts with you: your kids will follow the example you set.

- Notice when you've gone into fight-or-flight mode.

- Remember to breathe: it's the quickest way to calm down.

- Ask for help: be clear with others on the kind of support you need.

- Go easy on yourself: every parent feels like a failure sometimes.

Step
2

Break free from
worry and guilt

Our generation of parents is suffering from an epidemic of not feeling good enough. So many of the mums and dads I work with are extremely self-critical and judge themselves very harshly. I believe this is because most of us weren't brought up in households where our parents were kind to themselves. It's not our fault that we have inherited these patterns, but it is our job to change them so our own kids don't end up stuck in self-judgement and blame.

Why do we spend so much time beating ourselves up? From day one, we're programmed to believe we're not good enough. Since our earliest childhood, we've been set up to compete – bombarded with messages telling us that we need to achieve more, work harder, be thinner, look more attractive, earn more money and strive for perfection. When we become parents, the pressure to 'get it right' can seem overwhelming. The fact you've read this far is already proof that you care about being a good parent. But the 'inner critic' is so stubborn that if I even try to suggest to some parents that they are doing a much better job than they realize, they dismiss what I'm saying by waving a hand and telling me I'm just trying to be nice. I can almost see them thinking, 'That's all very well for you to say – but you wouldn't be so sympathetic if you saw just how impatient I can get with my kid sometimes.'

The problem doesn't stop there. As parents I work with begin to see how hard they can be on themselves, they often start beating themselves up over their habit of beating themselves up. Remember that this is a collective problem: every one of us struggles at some level with accepting ourselves, just as we are.

There is another way. We can start to develop a healthier relationship with our busy minds and all the many stories they tell us about how we have failed or not done well enough. We can realize that much of the time, the running commentary in our head that causes us so much misery isn't even true.

Filling in gaps

We've all had the experience of making a snap judgement about a situation or person, only to discover that our first impressions were wide of the mark. I saw this most clearly myself some years ago, when I had just qualified as a clinical psychologist. I was obsessing over a text from a boyfriend, coming up with all kinds of interpretations of what he might mean. My friend Kirsty turned to me in exasperation and said, 'You're filling in gaps.' And of course she was right. My mind had made up a story that I believed without question – but was it even true? I hadn't stopped to think. When we begin to examine our thoughts more closely, it can be quite a shock to realize how often our minds fill in gaps in this way, often worrying about things which may never happen, or inventing explanations that we later recognize don't fit the facts.

Of course, this is not to deny that problems do exist. It's completely normal for parents to worry, particularly when there are real concerns about their child. But worrying about what might happen in the future can easily take us over and make it harder to deal with the challenges we're actually facing in the here and now. We may think our worrying is helpful, but in reality it's mostly just draining us. Our own mind is behaving like a 'frenemy' living in our head.

Here's an example of what I mean. Let's imagine the following scenario. Say you receive a voicemail from your son's school asking you to call his head of year, but they don't say what it's about. Suddenly the gap-filling begins:

'What's happened to my son? Has he done something wrong? Is he in trouble? Has he forgotten to do his homework again?' Before you know it, the mind has created a worst-case scenario and you're frantic with worry. Ten minutes later, you get hold of the school and find out that all they wanted was to follow up on an innocent query related to a school trip. All the worry was caused by your mind going into overdrive. How often do we find ourselves caught in stories about ourselves or others that may not be true?

The more I worked with parents, the more I came to see that 'filling in gaps' is a universal problem. It's so automatic that we don't even notice our minds are doing it, constantly creating stories that often make us feel worse. Our minds are obviously wonderful tools – but they can easily lead us astray. Though the problems faced by families are very real, we often have more options at our disposal than we realize. We can learn to perceive our mental chatter for what it is: a stream of thinking that often misleads us, behaving more like a 'frenemy' than a helpful ally.

A new relationship with the 'frenemy'

Our minds are far more powerful than we often realize. Every second of the day, we're interpreting what is happening around us based on our past experiences, our upbringing, our personality and our beliefs. The way our minds filter what's happening makes all the difference between whether we often feel stressed and anxious or whether we're more able to accept life as it comes. Our habitual way of seeing the world is so familiar that we rarely pause to question how helpful it is.

When I work with parents, I often try a little experiment. I ask them to imagine that they are hooked up to a machine that records every single one of their thoughts over twenty-four hours. It would be like having a sort of internal PA who produces a written transcript of everything that's gone through your head. An excerpt from the transcript might look something like this:

> *'I can't believe I shouted at my kids again this morning. I bet no one else's kids have to hear their mother yelling at them before breakfast! I'm a bad mum – I'm failing my children. I really just need a bit of space – but there isn't time. I should get up an hour earlier – that would help me be more on top of everything. But I'm too tired to get up that early. I need to do better, be more organized and in control . . .'*

I then ask the parent to consider:

● How many thoughts does their twenty-four-hour transcript contain?

● How many of these thoughts were actually helpful?

● How many of these thoughts were critical of *you*?

Of course, the point is not to come up with precise answers, but to use these questions to start to appreciate just how busy our minds can get. It can be quite a surprise to realize what a chatterbox we have for company, and how often it decides to subject us to a barrage of criticism or blame. Some mums and dads break into a smile or even laugh out loud when they see this clearly. So much of the time, our thoughts are going around in circles, distracting us from what we're doing or putting a negative spin on things. It's no wonder so many of us feel worn-out, edgy and stressed.

The stream never stops. You could take a thirty-second section of the transcript from virtually any time of the day and the chances are that your mind would be feeding you a similar diet of thoughts – worrying about the to-do list, going over things that happened in the past or imagining what could go wrong in the future. We believe that we think our thoughts, but often our thoughts seem to be thinking us. What if we paused to look more closely? As we start to pay more attention, we may begin to understand that – at the deepest level – we are the *observer* of our mind, and not the stream of opinions, judgements and speculation it constantly pours forth.

The spiritual teacher Eckhart Tolle suggests another helpful exercise for stepping back from the stream of our habitual thinking in his excellent book *The Power of Now*. Imagine for a moment that you are a cat, waiting by a mousehole. Can you stay alert without thinking any thought at all? Or does a thought suddenly appear? What does the thought say? Where did it come from? Does it deserve to be taken seriously? Is it even true?

Tricks of the mind

Our negative patterns of thinking can be so familiar that we often assume that they are a fundamental part of who we are. On closer inspection, we may start to see them more as habits, much like biting our nails or smoking. Of course, habits are not always easy to break – but we can find ways to work with them.

To help us do this, researchers including Dr Aaron Beck and Dr David Burns have explored the way we are prone to falling into what psychologists call 'thinking traps' – typical ways in which our minds lose perspective and make a situation seem worse than it actually is. You may wish to ask yourself if any of the below seem familiar:

Common thinking traps

● **Black-and-white thinking.** No shades of grey: *'I'm the worst parent in the world. It's the one thing I should be able to do, and I can't. If I'm not perfect as a parent, I'm a complete failure.'*

Continued . . .

● **Catastrophizing.** Assuming the worst possible outcome: *'That's it, I lost it again. I have messed up my child for ever. They will hate me and have to spend the rest of their life in therapy – and they'll put all the blame on me.'*

● **Mind-reading.** Jumping to conclusions about what others are thinking, without any evidence: *'She's definitely judging me for deciding to send my children to private school.'*

● **'Should' statements.** Telling yourself how you 'should' or 'must' act: *'I've only got one child, but other parents with much bigger families are breezing through. I should be able to cope.'*

● **Focusing on negatives.** Dwelling on problems and downplaying positives: *'It doesn't matter that I've been calmer lately and things seem to be on a more even keel. The fact I lost it in the supermarket in front of everyone has ruined everything.'*

● **Disqualifying positives.** We discount the good things in our life and dismiss possibilities for improvement with: *'Yes, but . . .'*

● **Self-labelling.** Habitually calling ourselves names: *'I'm such an idiot. I'm a loser.' 'I'm so weak.' 'I'm such a mean dad.'*

- **Over-generalizing.** One bad thing happens and we say: *'My kids won't stop squabbling today: everything always goes wrong for me as a parent.'*

The 'frenemy' is a master story-teller

As we begin to notice how much of the time our mind is going over the same old ground, we may discover that the stories follow familiar themes – a little like the scripts of old movies we've seen a thousand times. Once we start to recognize them for what they are – just stories – their power over us begins to weaken. We begin to realize we don't need to believe everything our mind tells us. Here are some of the movie scripts I typically encounter with parents:

The 'guilt' script

This is a big one: so many parents tell me they are worried that they have failed their child in some way because of what they did or did not do. Every parent experiences a degree of guilt at some point in their life – it's a sign that you care about doing the best you can, and it can encourage you to make positive changes. But guilt becomes a problem when it starts to take over your life and you feel there's no way out. Here are some examples of the 'guilt script' in action:

'I feel terrible about sending my son to nursery because I had to go back to work. I know I spoil him to make it up to him, and that makes me feel even more guilty.'

'I get impatient with my daughter's constant questions and that makes me feel like a horrible parent.'

'I feel guilty for saying that I'm bored of taking my daughter to the swings for the ten millionth time when there are people who can't have children.'

'I feel guilty that I don't seem to be able to remain calm and composed and be a good role model for my son.'

'I feel guilty that I'm always arguing with my partner in front of the kids.'

'She's inherited all my anxiety and over-sensitivity.'

'I feel guilty for not feeling more gratitude when there are so many other families who are much worse off than us.'

'I feel guilty that I can't afford to send my daughters to dance lessons. They're missing out and it's my fault.'

'I feel terrible about the stress my youngest son faced as a baby: it was a difficult birth and I had post-natal depression. My other kids got a much more chilled-out mum.'

'I let them watch too much TV and don't play with them enough.'

'I don't feel particularly guilty when I leave them to go out and have some "me time", so I end up feeling guilty about not feeling guilty.'

'I feel guilty that their dad and I are not together any more.'

'I wish I'd been able to give each of my children more individual attention.'

'I experience guilt over the fact that I don't seem to be able to just be in the here and now and savour every moment I have with my children. I know these precious years are rushing by, and one day I will look back and wish I had enjoyed them more.'

Kelly: Too guilty for 'me time'

'My husband gave me a spa day for my birthday last summer but I haven't used it yet. It feels frivolous to spend a whole day away from the children faffing around in a dressing gown. But it would be really good for me to go – I really need some "me time", to moan with friends or just get a little bit of head space. I don't know why I feel

Continued . . .

> guilty. I don't know why I can't give myself permission to take a little time away. Since I do so much of the parenting, it's as if I've entered the mindset that I always have to do it all – and I feel guilty if anyone else does anything. Handing over control is hard. I am a control freak. I always have been. I even feel guilty if my mum picks up the kids for me – I worry: will they behave? It's hard to let go.'

The 'being judged' script

It's very common for parents to feel they're being judged by other parents, or by their own parents and in-laws, who are convinced they know the 'right' way to raise children. Of course, we can all be a little judgy at times – it's part of human nature – and most of us are our own harshest critic. However, if you're feeling under attack from others, bear in mind that the opinions of those who would pass judgement reveal a lot more about them than they do about you. Here are some examples of the 'being judged' script in action:

> 'I'm scared my child's birthday party won't measure up.'

> 'I'm a working mum and I'm sure other parents think I don't spend enough time with my children.'

'I'm a stay-at-home mum and I feel like people see me as a second-class citizen.'

'I thought that as a woman I knew what it was to be judged, but I realized I didn't really know what that meant until I became a mum. It seems like everyone has an opinion on how best to raise your child!'

'My mother's always criticizing the way I discipline my kids – she says I'm too soft and I let them spend too much time on the iPad or in front of the TV.'

'Now I'm a parent, I will never judge another parent again – you don't know what they've had to deal with all day.'

Karen: 'I know I shouldn't compare myself'

'I'm so scared of being judged that my stress levels are through the roof and everything has to be "just right". We've just been on a family holiday to Spain, which should have been a relaxing break, but I was so het up about making everything perfect and trying to make sure that everyone else had a good time that I couldn't relax and enjoy the holiday. I was on edge the whole time and kept bursting into tears. I know I shouldn't, but I can't

Continued . . .

> *stop judging myself harshly compared with the other mums at Mark's school. I had some of them round for dinner a few weeks ago and I nearly had a panic attack trying to make sure everything was absolutely perfect. I found it all very exhausting. I wish I could just learn to stop worrying about what other people think.'*

The 'what if' script

Worry is perhaps the most common script of all. It's a given that as a parent you're going to worry more – whether you experience nagging 'what if' thoughts or find yourself constantly contemplating worst-case scenarios. Often the most caring people worry the most. However, worrying can be exhausting and counter-productive when it goes round in endless circles without leading to constructive action:

'What if my son's under too much pressure at school?'

'I'm worried about whether my kids are going to turn out okay.'

'What if my son's spending too much time on his Xbox?'

'I worry my daughter's got into the wrong crowd.'

'Since we've had kids our relationship's not been the same.'

'What if we've chosen the wrong school?'

'I'm worried my teenage son is unable to take responsibility for basic things like his homework and household chores.'

'What if my kids only remember the stressful times, even though I've tried my best to make it up to them?'

Dave: 'I'm worried about going back to work full-time'

'I find it hard to sleep at night because I'm not sure I made the right decision to go back to work full-time. Maybe it will affect my bond with Kayleigh, my seven-year-old, if I'm not at home with the family so much? But we really need the money, and I need a different focus and the adult company.'

Flipping the script

As we become more familiar with our 'frenemy's' favourite movie scripts, a new question arises: now what?

The first thing to remember is that we can't just get rid

of our 'negative' thoughts – and fighting them just makes them worse. It's an old psychologist's cliché to point out that if I say, 'Don't think of a pink elephant,' then one will inevitably pop into your mind's eye. That's just the way the brain works. Trying to stop your thoughts is like trying to stop waves on the ocean with a pane of glass. The good news is that even noticing that you are replaying an old script will make it easier to start to look at things in a more resourceful way. Some parents find the following exercises useful:

- **Write the storyline down.** When I was going through a phase of high anxiety a few years ago, I found it very helpful to write the content of my worry on my smartphone. For example: 'I am feeling like I'm wasting my life and always seem to be behind on everything.' Some parents use a diary or notebook to catalogue their worries, and this can be a surprisingly effective way to weaken their intensity (so much so that there are entire schools of psychotherapy based on writing).

- **Visualize releasing the story.** Some parents imagine pinning their worries, guilt script or feelings of being judged on to a passing cloud, placing them gently on a leaf floating by on a stream or launching them to a distant star. You might also experiment with visualizing negative feelings as train passengers and watch them step off your carriage before you continue with your journey. Or you could try waving goodbye to your 'frenemy' and all the angst it causes.

- **Turn down the volume.** Just as we can turn down the volume on a news channel pumping out depressing stories that we can't immediately do anything about, we can make a conscious choice to turn down the volume on our worries. It can be helpful to visualize turning down a radio to reduce the intensity of negative thoughts – and then adjust the dial to a station with more positive messages.

Working with worry

There's a reason why thinking positively can seem so difficult. Our brains have evolved to focus on potential threats; if they hadn't then our ancestors wouldn't have lasted very long. Worrying about being attacked by wild animals or running out of food – rather than stopping to smell the flowers or appreciate the sunset – is what has kept our species alive. We've inherited the same negative bias. Given the amount of responsibility parents have and the number of tasks they're facing each day, worry is inevitable. As many parents tell me, 'Worrying is what helps me to be caring and responsible and keep my family safe. If I don't worry, who will?'

Worry is good if it really is helping us to solve problems or take helpful action. The problems start when our worry gets so out of hand that it begins to consume our day-to-day lives and leave us feeling anxious and drained. We can find ourselves covering the same ground over and over again, without really getting anywhere. It's like following well-worn tracks on a ski slope: we fall into the same old grooves without realizing there may be another path we can take. There's a big difference between sitting down to solve a problem and going round and round in circles worrying about all the bad things that could happen that you can't control. Many of us worry that we can't seem to stop worrying. It's easy to start feeling helpless.

The goal is not to fight our thoughts and feelings, but gradually to change our relationship with them. We begin to examine whether a particular pattern of thought is serving us and whether there might be other perspectives we can consider. Of course, this isn't always easy – and the mind loves nothing more than to tell us that we can't step back from our thoughts, and that we might as well give up trying. The trick is to start to see these thoughts as just another unhelpful script.

When we find ourselves in the grip of worries, it can help to reflect on the following questions:

- Is this a pressing problem or a hypothetical 'what if' issue?

- Is there something I can do about this right now?

- Does it make more sense to plan to tackle this in the future?

These questions can help us start to draw a clearer distinction between the constructive process of carefully and calmly thinking through a problem, and the 'frenemy's' tendency to dwell on worst-case scenarios or point an accusing finger of self-blame.

Jennifer: 'I'm learning to catch my thoughts'

'The worst times are at bedtime and in the mornings. Sometimes Liam seems okay, but more and more he doesn't seem to listen to anything I say. He always seems to be playing games on his phone and if I try to set limits or give him instructions he says really horrible things to me. I almost can't believe it's coming from the mouth of a nine-year-old, especially my own son. I try to get him to do his homework, but he refuses – and I find myself losing my temper. Then I feel terrible afterwards and worry that I'm turning into one of those awful "shouty" mums. Nothing could have prepared me for how stressful being a mum is – my mind's just constantly on overdrive. I have a million thoughts a day – it's so crazy and manic.

Continued . . .

I feel like I'm going insane sometimes. I keep bursting into tears. I can't stop worrying and thinking the worst.'

At first, Jennifer cries as she tells her story, feeling frustrated and ashamed. I work with her to help her to become more aware of what she's thinking. When she's starting to feel upset, she silently asks, *'What's going on in my mind right now?'*

Jennifer gradually starts to notice how often she seeks to push away her difficult thoughts and feelings by keeping constantly busy or drinking one or two extra glasses of wine. She identifies the following themes: *'I've ruined everything. I'm a bad mum. Everyone's better than me.'*

As Jennifer learns to step back from her busy mind, she starts to catch herself when an old 'script' has begun to play. She makes a note of her thoughts on her phone, which helps her to see them more objectively. She also learns to express appreciation for her mind, despite the pain it causes, which helps her to avoid being too harsh on herself.

Jennifer makes a point of taking five deep breaths – during her commute, at the office, when she's cooking and while she's lying in bed at night. She likes to silently say the word 'calm' as she's breathing out. She starts to notice when she's going around in circles, and gets better at remembering to pause and ask, *'Is this something I can do anything about right now? Are these thoughts taking me anywhere?'*

Gradually, Jennifer starts to feel calmer and finds that her negative thoughts don't have quite so much power. She is able to see that her old 'scripts' are just stories – not necessarily facts. Her son senses the shift and over time their relationship improves.

'I'm able to say, "Ah, okay – I'm getting really angry here",' Jennifer says. *'I ask myself, "Can I take a few deep breaths before I say or do anything I might regret?" I'm recognizing I've got more options than I realize. I don't have to act so impulsively, or to take my mind quite so seriously.'*

Towards a deeper connection

As we begin to develop more awareness of our habitual thoughts, and find little gaps in our stream of thinking, something remarkable starts to happen. We naturally start to question whether the stories we've always believed about ourselves are actually true. We may start to feel a greater sense of trust – in ourselves, and in life. We may find we are less in thrall to habits that no longer serve us. And we start to speak, think and act from a deeper, more confident place. Each time you remember to pause and take a breath, you're nurturing the seed of calm which we all carry within us, but with which we can easily lose touch in the busyness of day-to-day parenting.

We may notice that each time we connect with this deeper part of ourselves, we feel a greater sense of connection to others – no matter how different they appear on the surface, whether in terms of their appearance or the way they live their lives. Most importantly, we also sense a deeper connection with our children. We might still get angry if they've just spilled their juice all over our new carpet or slammed their bedroom door, but we never lose touch with the unconditional bond we share.

When we start to feel this connection more regularly, we may experience a sense of altruism that goes far beyond our initial goal of feeling a little better in ourselves. We may be more inclined to share a smile, a kind gesture or even a more ambitious contribution to our family, our community or the wider world. And we tend to have greater confidence in our ability to choose an effective response to our everyday parenting dilemmas – whether it's a son in the midst of a meltdown or a daughter who's refusing to speak.

The five key points

Break free from worry and guilt

- Our busy minds can make parenting harder than it needs to be.

- Taking a deep breath gives us a chance to respond rather than react.

- If you're worrying, ask yourself: 'am I filling in gaps?'.

- We all get caught in the same old scripts: learn to spot them.

- The mind is a master story-teller: don't believe everything it says.

Trust yourself

Every parent has heard the saying that it takes a village to raise a child. In tribal societies, boys and girls were expected to start contributing to their community as soon as they could walk – fetching water, foraging for nuts and berries or looking after their even tinier siblings. The whole concept of 'childhood' as we know it today is a relative newcomer on the stage, and the conventional wisdom about how best to bring up children seems to change with each passing decade.

We can all picture a stern Victorian parent insisting that children should be seen and not heard. Even as late as 1928, the influential American psychologist John B. Watson wrote a popular book called *Psychological Care of Infant and Child* in which he advised parents to withhold affection so as not to 'spoil' their children. He believed that the ideal version of the parent–child relationship should be cool and businesslike – perhaps best symbolized by his recommendation to parents to dress their children like adults and shake hands with them each morning.

By the end of the Second World War, attitudes had started to shift. The renowned paediatrician Dr Benjamin Spock encouraged mothers to leave stern Victorian attitudes behind and be as generous as possible with their warmth and love. Though controversial in many respects, Spock's *Baby and Child Care*, published in 1946, became one of the bestselling books of all time. Spock's emphasis on parental instincts and intuition shapes attitudes to this day. In the 1950s, John Bowlby's seminal research on 'attachment' demonstrated the importance of the mother–child bond for a child's healthy emotional development and cemented the move away from the strict, punitive parenting school of the previous century.

Since then, an array of new styles has developed, each championed by different experts – from the relaxed and flexible 'permissive parenting' of the 1960s to the rise of the more strategy-based techniques of the 'naughty step' and 'reward charts' popularized in more recent years. We can all now agree that kids need limits and boundaries to feel safe – but, equally, there's a growing recognition that not all strategies will work for all children at all times. Nobody denies the importance of an emotional connection with our children and the need to give them space to express their unique identity. At the same time, the wealth of choices to make and the deluge of information on offer poses parents with new dilemmas. Nobody wants to turn the clock back, but how do we know we're doing the right thing?

I recently met a mum who voiced concerns I've heard many times in my work with parents. She was so committed to getting her relationship with her son exactly 'right' that she found herself constantly assailed by worries about what might – or might not – be going on in his head. She experienced a stream of thoughts such as: 'I feel there's something he's not telling me. Does he even like me? I've not got the emotional connection "right".' It was almost as if parenting was an exam that she absolutely had to pass. It's not hard to imagine how exhausting this burden of self-doubt was to live with on a daily basis. The sad thing is that this kind of parental anxiety can easily prove contagious – slowly weakening the very connection that this mum was so desperate to preserve.

If this kind of dilemma sounds familiar in any way, you may wish to take a moment to consider some of the following questions:

- Do I worry about whether I'm a good enough role model?

- Do I feel guilty in some way about my performance as a parent – for example, am I afraid that I'm being either too weak or too dictatorial?

- Do I ever worry about what my child thinks of me?

- How good am I at setting boundaries and sticking to them?

- Does my child ever seem overwhelmed by the choices I am giving them?

- How easy do I find it to say 'no' to my child?

- Do I often question whether I am doing enough to support my child?

I hear parents asking these kinds of questions all the time, and I often wonder: why are we so hard on ourselves? Perhaps it has something to do with the many voices at work in the back of our minds as we bring up our children. When we start our journey as parents, we are never alone. Friends, family, teachers and health professionals all offer well-intentioned suggestions on the choices we should make and tips for dealing with our child's inevitable growing pains. Aside from this avalanche of advice, there is another influence at work that may have a far bigger impact than even those closest to us: the parenting script we acquired during our own childhood.

All of us have absorbed ideas about what it means to be a mum or dad from the way we were brought up. When we have children, these ideas may influence our own parenting style without us even realizing it. We can easily find ourselves reacting to challenges just like our own parents did – especially when we are feeling pressured, or facing a situation similar to something that happened in our own early life.

Of course, many of the positive values we've inherited have uplifted us and enriched our own family's lives. But there are times when running on our default setting does not serve us and we may find ourselves reacting in unhelpful ways. This is the moment to step back and consult what I call the 'inner parent' – a source of innate wisdom that we all carry within. This is the part of us that knows how to respond to any given situation – if we can take a moment to pause and listen. By tapping into this guidance, we feel more confident and can respond to the challenges we face every day as parents in new, more creative ways.

The 'inner parent': trusting your instincts

In everyday life there are clear rules to follow: at school, at work, in social situations, in driving our cars and in the payment of our taxes. The same does not hold true for raising children. Many books offer parents strategies, techniques and step-by-step guides, and you may find they contain valuable tools that work for you and your child. However, the ultimate authority on your daughter or son is you – and the goal of this book is to encourage you to cultivate your own guidance. With a little practice, we can all learn to tune in to the voice of the 'inner parent'. Although we may sometimes forget to consult it, the voice never gives up on us – and over time it will be easier to hear whenever we stop and take five deep breaths, pause, quieten our mind and listen.

Most of us have had an experience of instinctively know-ing that something was the right thing to do without necessarily being able to explain why. We might call it an 'intuition' or a 'flash' of insight – knowledge delivered to us from beyond our day-to-day thinking mind. Almost by def-inition, these are unusual occurrences and most of us don't experience them on any consistent basis. All too often, these messages from our 'inner parent' are drowned out by all the distractions of modern life and of course, that ever-present 'frenemy' in our head who chips away at us and undermines our confidence. It can therefore be a little irritating when somebody says just 'follow your gut' or 'trust your instincts' as if it were as easy as reading an email or opening a letter.

On the other hand, we may have a strong instinct that something's not right – but our 'frenemy' mind starts to question what our intuition is telling us and we end up going around in circles. It's not always easy to hear what our 'inner parent' is saying. But there is an emerging body of scientific research that suggests our intuition is far from 'all in the mind'.

Brain, heart and gut

As we saw in Step 2, for most of us, our attention is so caught up in the stream of thinking in our head that we don't pay much attention to what our body is telling us. But researchers are gradually coming round to the idea that listening to our 'gut feelings' or 'following our heart' has a much firmer basis in biology than we might assume.

Scientists used to think that the major organs were controlled by the brain – viewed as a kind of central computer sending instructions to the body below. We now know that things are a lot more complicated than that. Both the gut and the heart have their own 'little brains' – intricate networks of neurons, neurotransmitters, proteins and support cells similar to those found in the brain proper, but functioning largely independently. Indeed, research by the HeartMath Institute in California has shown that the heart produces an electromagnetic field a hundred times more powerful than that of the brain. The field radiates outside the body three feet in every direction and seems to influence other people, even our pets.

The Vagus – the nerve that starts at the base of the skull and meanders through our body – may also play a bigger role in our decision-making than we might imagine. Researchers have discovered that 80 per cent of the Vagus's bandwidth is taken up carrying signals from the body *to* the brain. In a very real sense, we are constantly being fed information by our gut and heart, and these signals seem to play a very significant role in how we think, feel and react.

*

Louise: 'I started listening to myself more'

'When you first have a child, you have no idea what you are doing. Being a mum wasn't instinctive, or intuitive and didn't come naturally to me. I felt like a failure, disempowered and helpless most of the time. I questioned everything I was doing very early on with my daughter, and I just wanted someone to tell me what to do – to give me concrete answers. Although Dr Google and advice from friends and family were helpful at times, sometimes all this information made me doubt myself even more. If you're already a little under-confident, then parenting can play into all those existing insecurities. The parenting industry also dishes out so much fear and anxiety to parents.

'In the end, I got post-natal depression and a lot of anxiety from all the conflicting advice I was reading in books. Everyone seems to tell you something different. People were always trying to make me feel a bit better, and would say to look on the bright side, which only made me feel worse. I had done very well in my job and was always super-organized. Once I had my daughter, everything felt so out of control.

'Fast forward a few years: I am now well again. My home basically looks like a bomb has hit it, but I've

Continued . . .

> *learned to be okay with that. What changed? Well, I started listening to myself more, and tapped in to my intuition. I found that I had an inner voice guiding me all along.'*

As parents, what do we value?

Our culture tends to place a great deal of emphasis on goals – specific things we want to do, be or have in the future. We don't tend to reflect so much on our values – the qualities we want to embody as we go about our daily lives. Goals might be our destination, but values are all about the way we make the journey. For example, one parent may see discipline, order and achievement as very important. Another may place more emphasis on a sense of adventure, laughter and freedom.

Working out the values we prize most highly is not hard – you just need to take a moment to reflect. From our earliest childhood, all of us have absorbed values from other people: our parents, relatives, teachers, the place we live and the media. But there comes a time when we might want to explore what's most important to *us*, rather than following the norms we internalized without question as we grew up. Reflecting on the values you hold most dear is a sure-fire way to build a closer relationship with your 'inner parent' and stay true to yourself.

This is not just an academic exercise. Making an effort to identify our values and starting to live more in alignment with them can help our experience as parents to unfold with greater harmony. To take a simple example, if one of your most important values is spending time with family, but you are devoting seventy hours a week to a demanding job, then you will feel constantly stressed. Equally, if you place a high value on connecting with nature and recognize the pleasure it brings you, but you rarely visit the countryside, you won't feel your best. Exploring your values helps you to make better decisions – and to be clearer about the kinds of qualities you want to encourage in your children.

I find investigating values is one of the most fruitful avenues in my work with parents. No matter what has happened in the past, it's always possible to get clear in your mind what's important to you now. You can then begin to take small steps towards living your values more fully – and feel more confident as a result.

Let's try it now. There's some inspiration in the words below. Scan through them quickly and pick out the first three that leap out at you:

independence curiosity **adventure** enthusiasm

humour playfulness **respect**

courage authenticity **integrity** knowledge

honesty **creativity** appreciation

diversity order **discipline** nature vitality

collaboration spirituality beauty *sensuality*

humility **achievement** intimacy community

resilience fairness **freedom** compassion

forgiveness open-mindedness **tolerance**

romance expression **generosity**

financial security cooperation *gratitude*

When you've settled on your top three values, have a think about how far they are present in your day-to-day life as a parent. For example, let's say you chose the words 'cooperation', 'collaboration' and 'community'. Try to think of some recent examples of how you felt you were cooperating with other parents, or contributing to a community, such as your child's school. It can be really life-affirming to acknowledge the extent to which you are already living these values – perhaps in ways you hadn't really acknowledged before. Equally, you may feel you could be expressing your chosen values more fully. In the case of 'collaboration', perhaps you're keen to forge a closer approach to parenting with your partner. As you reflect on your relationship with your values, it might help to consider some of the following questions:

- What kinds of actions could you take or activities could you pursue that would bring more of these qualities into your everyday experience?

- How much time and energy are you devoting to cultivating your values? What changes could you make? Think about how your values are present in specific areas: family life, relationships, work and leisure.

- Have a discussion with your family about your family's 'core values'.

- Encourage your partner and family members to make their own lists.

- Consider how your list may have been different ten years ago.

- Think about ways in which you'd like to foster your values in the way you interact with your child.

Jo: 'I can't change my son – but I can change how I treat myself'

'You feel like you should be enjoying these years, but my fourteen-year-old, Jamie, is just such a nightmare sometimes. I wish he would show me some appreciation, but I wonder if I'm being needy and my expectations are maybe too high. My mother always told me life isn't fair – and I've grown up to see she was right. I just want to find a way to enjoy life a bit more again without all the battles and stress.'

We talk about Jo's values and come up with:

● **Appreciation.** *'If I was appreciated, Jamie would say thank you for everything I do for him. As it stands, I don't feel like he has any idea about the sacrifices I've made.'*

● **Humour.** *'We don't have a laugh any more – it's all about having to discipline Jamie. He's always being rude and complaining. I could just do with a giggle with girlfriends – a little light relief from all the tension.'*

● **Fairness.** *'For me, it's about things feeling equal – some give and take. At the moment I feel like I'm drained from just giving – it doesn't feel fair. But I know I shouldn't resent looking after my own son.'*

We talk about what seems to be getting in the way of Jo expressing these values in her daily life: *'If I'm honest, although I want Jamie to say "thank you", I probably don't express that clearly – I mainly just shout. I find it difficult to spell out what I want. It doesn't come naturally to me to speak up because I've always been so busy looking after everyone else. There doesn't seem to be any time to just have fun.'*

Jo and I discuss the kinds of small, deliberate steps she could take to start embodying her values in daily life, rather than looking for them from her son.

● **Appreciation.** *'I'm beginning to see that I could start to show more appreciation for myself, rather than waiting for affirmation from outside. I could start a gratitude journal and use it to check in with myself to see what's gone well each day and how I've handled situations. If I could make this into a habit, it would remind me to appreciate myself more, rather than always waiting for validation and "thank-you"s from others.'*

● **Humour.** *'I could get myself one of the comedy box sets I really used to love. I can't remember the last time I hugged my son or sat down together to watch something funny on TV. He seems so grown up now, but I know he's not too old to enjoy a laugh with his mum.'*

Continued . . .

● **Fairness.** *'Fairness is about people treating me properly. I've realized I need to look at my boundaries. If I'm honest, I've always been a bit of a doormat. I tend to say "yes" to everything and then end up feeling resentful. Maybe I could come to an agreement with Jamie to share some of the housework.'*

Jo says, *'I know I can't change my son overnight – but I can change the way I treat myself.'*

When our buttons are being pushed – and what we can learn from it

As any parent knows, children are experts at pressing our buttons. It's almost as if they arrive pre-programmed to get a reaction out of us, and will keep going relentlessly or refuse to do what they're told until we either give in to their demands or lose our temper. In an instant, we go from being calm and clear-headed to agitated, anxious or angry, or feeling sensitive and upset. You may hear yourself snapping or shouting at them without even knowing where the harsh words came from, or why you are suddenly boiling over. In these flashpoints, any hope of taking a pause to consult your 'inner parent' goes out of the window. When you've had time to calm down, you may see on a logical level that your reaction was out of proportion, but at the time it was impossible to keep your emotions under control.

Becca: 'My daughter's always slagging me off'

'From the moment I open my eyes, my eight-year-old, Jasmine, starts having a go at me. I'm a single parent and she likes to say, "No one will ever want you" and points out my grey hairs. Jasmine's very critical of me. At the swimming pool, I told her to stop pulling our clothes bag around, and then everything fell out all over the place. She said, "It's your f—ing fault," and we had a major meltdown there and then. Once, when we were having an argument, Jasmine looked at me and made a gesture as if pulling string out of her ears. I asked what she was doing and she said, "I'm pulling all my happy memories of us out of my brain." I felt shocked and genuinely hurt that my daughter could say such a thing. If you're feeling buoyant then it's okay, and somehow you can excuse things like this. But when you're feeling fairly low it's horrible to have to listen to it. I just don't know what's going on with her.'

Strong reactions can be a sign that something from our past is playing out in the here and now. The key is to start to see these moments as opportunities to learn more about ourselves, rather than as yet more reasons to beat ourselves up. We begin to approach such flashpoints with curiosity, pausing to investigate what is happening inside our bodies and minds, rather than trying to push our thoughts and sensations away. As we feel our frustration rising, we maintain an awareness of what we're thinking and feeling. As we learn to observe our reactions in the moment – as they are occurring – they begin to lose their power.

As we become more familiar with the feelings that go with the messier side of parenting, it can help to cast our minds back to reflect a little on what went on during our own childhoods. Whether we remember it fondly or otherwise, our own upbringing will inevitably have shaped our approach to parenting. We may be grateful for what we've learned, or we may want to avoid repeating our parents' mistakes – or a bit of both. Many of us can recognize our own mum's or dad's habitual phrases in the ventriloquist's voice of our 'inner critic' when it says things like, 'There you go, messing things up again!' or 'Why couldn't you have tried just a bit harder?' After telling off our children, we might catch ourselves thinking, 'I sound just like my mum.'

Parents I work with can often be very surprised when they suddenly realize quite how much their upbringing has shaped their reactions to the challenges they encounter while raising their own kids. You might also be able to see a clear link between episodes from your own childhood and your parenting style. If you want to look into this more deeply, try scanning the following list of statements to see if any of them remind you of your own early life:

- We didn't talk about feelings in our house.

- It was rare to show affection through touching or hugs.

- We always made sure we sat down together at mealtimes.

- We didn't do conflict and we were always polite.

- The only way to get noticed was by shouting or door-slamming.

- Crying was seen as a weakness.

- Our parents often showed their appreciation for one another.

- Education was a priority; it was all about good grades.

- We often talked about feelings in an open way.

- We felt controlled regarding our choices in education or in our careers.

- Everyone's voice was heard.

- We were allowed to do whatever we wanted with few limits.

- Our parents were always too busy to pay us much attention.

- Mum/Dad made all the decisions and there were no arguments.

- Our parents were always arguing.

- Mum/Dad always insisted everything was great — even if it wasn't.

Parental Voices

- James, a dad of three: *'Looking back, my mum was often depressed and she was constantly criticizing herself and everyone around her. She found it very difficult to be optimistic, and tended to have a very gloomy view of the world. She was a "glass half empty" type of person. I can easily find myself slipping into being very negative and I always seem to be beating myself up about my performance as a parent.'*

- Pippa, a mum of two: *'I pride myself on being generally a "together", smart and sensible mum, but there are times when I just seem to lose the plot and start yelling when my son and daughter start playing up — when they don't want to do their homework or are generally being uncooperative. For the longest time, I couldn't understand what was happening — until one day it hit me: "I sound just like my mother." I remember how my own mum used to go ballistic at me and my brothers,*

> *and then there'd be hell to pay when Dad finally got*
> *home from work. Sometimes we'd get a slap.'*
>
> ● Mike, a dad of one: *'I remember my dad as being*
> *very harsh and angry and he often drank too much. He*
> *used to come in and shout at everyone. I guess it's fair to*
> *say I grew up as a worrier. I can see my son is also quite*
> *anxious and I can't help blaming myself.'*

We can't change the past, but we can learn to spot when we're reacting in ways that echo how our parents treated us – and themselves. Our early experiences have such a strong impact that it's not always easy to be objective about them and they can easily drown out what our 'inner parent' might be trying to tell us. But if we can start to remember to pause, take five deep breaths and choose our response – rather than acting on autopilot – we'll feel more in control.

If you want to take a closer look at how your parental voices may still be active, it might help to consider some common triggers and responses:

Parental challenge in the present	How the challenge reminds me of my own childhood	How the challenge makes me feel now	What happens when I react without thinking
My kids are squabbling.	My parents used to argue all the time.	Tense; as if I'm about to explode with anger.	I shut down emotionally and withdraw.
My teenage son ignores me and keeps texting as I'm talking.	I often felt ignored as a child and that my parents weren't interested in me.	Rejected and sad; a sinking feeling in my stomach.	I get upset and start shouting to get my son's attention.
My daughter refuses to do what she's told.	My dad was strict and gave me very little freedom as a teenager.	Angry and overwhelmed; a tightness in my chest.	I shout and scream, then slam the door behind me.
My son throws a tantrum in the supermarket and won't stop screaming.	I never felt like I fitted in at school and always worried about being judged.	Anxious and embarrassed; fear of being seen as a bad parent.	I give in to my son's demands because I'm worried about what others think of me.

Mo: 'I'm now learning that I'm an adult'

'My own mum's voice is so ingrained in me that for years I made parenting decisions based on what I imagined she would say. Her voice in my head says things like, "If you do it in that way . . . Or if you did it like this . . . then it would be so much better for their education."

'Even though I'm a fully grown adult, I still feel I have to justify things in terms of what my mother would think. But as the years have gone by, I have come to realize that my mum's values are at odds with my own. I have to trust that I have my own set of values and my own way of doing things – and although my decisions may not always be right, I have to make my own mistakes and learn from them.'

Mo and I discuss the concept of 'mistakes'. It's easy with hindsight to look back and think you should have done something differently. But so much of the time we only truly change when things seem to go wrong in some way. So are our mistakes really mistakes – or opportunities to learn?

'I have a constant battle inside myself,' Mo says. 'Do I follow what she says? Or do I break free from the imprint of my mum's voice? I have listened to it a lot over the course of my life, but it's a new thing for me to be so

Continued . . .

aware of it. Now, when I hear her voice, I say, "That's my mum's voice; it's not mine." The more aware I am, the greater the choice I have over whether to follow it or not. I now realize that my mum doesn't always know best. I tell myself, "Be strong in what you think and what you believe." I am now learning that I am an adult and I have to take responsibility for the choices I make.

'I see an image of a bookshelf in a library. And I can now shelve the thoughts that belong to my mum. I thank her. If I want I can go back to the book with her thought in it and ask myself, is that helpful? Or does it make me doubt myself? What is right for me? What is right for my family?

'I realize now there isn't a "right" thing. It is listening to my intuition that is important. I make my own decisions now – and they're for me, not for Mum, or anybody else.'

No such thing as perfect

Every mum and dad wants to do the best they can, and it's easy to blame ourselves when we feel we're not getting it 'right'. But there's no such thing as perfect when it comes to parenting. We learn the most during the challenges and the hard times – when we fall down and pick ourselves up. As we gradually become more comfortable with the inevitable messiness, we survive the lows and relish the highs. This is the journey that makes us stronger and wiser, and teaches us that our children are here to help us learn the greatest lesson of all: to trust ourselves.

The five key points
Trust yourself

● You are the ultimate authority
on your kids: trust your 'inner parent'.

● When our kids push our buttons it
can be a sign that something from our
past is playing out in the here and now.

● Explore how your childhood has
shaped your parenting style.

● We can choose to parent in
line with our own values.

● Every parent is doing their
best: there's no such
thing as perfect.

Step
4

Connect with your child every day

There are times when parents experience a profound sense of connection with their child – a priceless bond they would not sacrifice for anything. But there can also be moments when your child's constant demands for attention are so exhausting that you wonder how you'll cope. A gulf seems to open and any sense of harmony vanishes in the midst of arguments, tantrums, angry exchanges or sulking. Drained by your child's behaviour, and desperate to make them behave at any cost, it's easy to resort to threats or bribes. When these backfire, your son or daughter only becomes more argumentative or withdrawn. It feels as if something infinitely precious has been lost – and it's easy to worry that you won't get it back.

In these moments, we need to restore the Humility,

Empathy, Authenticity, Respect and Trust that make up the HEART-centred connection we discussed in the introduction. Building, nurturing and strengthening this connection is the most important thing we do as parents but it can also feel like one of the hardest.

Your relationship with your child is the foundation for everything. As babies, we are completely dependent on our parents. Our very survival depends on forming a loving bond with an adult. Psychologists call this bonding process 'attachment'. Plenty of research shows that forming a secure attachment is one of the most important factors that will influence a child's well-being in later life. But the importance of attachment does not stop when babies become toddlers: the parent–child relationship lasts a lifetime, and every single one of us needs close connections throughout our lives.

Building and maintaining a healthy attachment with our child takes work. We all love our children, but we cannot take our relationship with our child for granted. Like any relationship, we need to make it a priority if we want it to flourish. We need to put the time and effort in so that our children can learn to trust us, and feel safe in the knowledge that we are there for them.

We will soon know if our relationship with our child is breaking down. I have worked with many parents who feel desperate and don't know what to do about their child. Perhaps they have a 10-year-old son who ignores everything his mother tells him and just keeps playing on his Xbox. Or maybe they have a 15-year-old daughter who stays out late with her friends, driving her dad frantic with worry, and then refuses to say where she has been. The symptoms may be different, but the underlying cause of these problems is the same: a loss of connection. When our kids act up or challenge us in some way, we have to start by looking at our relationship with them and asking: do my children feel connected to me?

Kids will always push boundaries – that's a normal part of learning to be independent. Just because a child seems to be behaving badly doesn't mean our relationship is broken. But we do need to do what we can to maintain a healthy connection. When our children can find connection to us in their daily lives, they are less likely to act out to gain our attention, and more likely to turn to us for support, guidance and love.

Now let's talk about how we can make our connection stronger.

Make connecting a daily habit

No matter what's happened in the past, we can always cultivate a closer relationship with our kids. We don't have to set aside huge blocks of time: there are so many opportunities to make a meaningful connection every day. We can enjoy early morning snuggles, or make a special effort to chat during the drive to school, the walk to the bus stop or after dinner.

For younger children, one of the best ways to strengthen your connection is through daily play. Take time to get down to their level on the floor and play with them for five minutes. Allow them to lead and direct what you do: this is about connecting with your child, not about teaching them to do something 'right'. You don't need expensive toys: simple things like blocks, cars, trucks and dolls are perfect. You can turn routine activities such as getting dressed, brushing teeth, and getting ready for bed into games. Create special characters or use silly voices. Not only will this build your relationship, it will make these kinds of routine activities more enjoyable.

Remember: even if play can feel repetitious, it is your kids' idea of fun. The time you invest will help them feel more connected, which in turn will make them happier and more cooperative, and the whole job of parenting so much easier.

Reading with your kids is another excellent way to strengthen your connection: it represents regular, uninterrupted time where your child knows they are going to get your complete focus. The sensations of being held by you and hearing your voice help your child's brain development and nurtures feelings of trust and safety as you share a magical journey into the imagination. Each time you read together, you help your child to develop the ability to imagine how someone else is feeling and to respond with care. You can ask them to pretend to put themselves in the shoes of a character and ask: 'How would they feel if that had happened to you? What would make you feel better if you were character X?' You can help your child develop emotional skills by asking them to make faces to show how they think the different characters in the story might be feeling.

The most important thing is to be fully present during these activities, so that your child can sense your genuine interest in them. With the pressures of modern life, and the constant lure of our phones, tablets and laptops, it's easy to be somewhere else, even when we are in the same room. How often do we find ourselves saying: 'I'll be with you in just a minute?' Take a moment to reflect on how you interact with your kids during an average day. How often are you really there?

This isn't about putting even more pressure on yourself or going on a guilt trip. You don't have to pay full attention to your kids 100 per cent of the time: it's all about balance. The more work you put into maintaining a healthy connection, the easier it will be to manage the conflicts or power struggles that happen in every family. Here are some practical tips for connecting in daily life:

- **Let your child express all their feelings.** By providing a safe space for your kids to say how they really feel, you will strengthen your bond.

- **Slow down and enjoy the good times.** Kids seem to grow up far too fast. As we prepare for the next phase or developmental milestone, it's important to remind ourselves that the moment we are in together now will not come again.

● **Make one-to-one time.** If you have more than one child schedule time with each of them separately — even fifteen minutes can make a big difference.

● **Put devices away.** Kids hate it when they have to compete for attention with a smartphone.

● **Hugs and snuggles.** First thing in the morning, last thing at night and any other time of the day: hugging your child builds connection. Remember that older children, although they may want less hugs, still need to feel close to you.

● **Bedtime chats.** These can be good moments to encourage your child to open up and share any worries that may be niggling them.

● **Read with your kids.** Reading can be an important part of a bedtime routine, and helps to settle them down at the end of a busy day.

● **Greet them properly after school.** It only takes a few moments to welcome your child home with genuine enthusiasm and ask them about the day, but this can make a huge difference in showing them that they are loved.

Canadian psychologist Gordon Neufeld believes that the way many of us live our lives today creates repeated experiences of separation for our young children, rather than experiences that bond us. When this happens too often our children can lose trust in us and our relationship can suffer. Think about how you say goodbye and how you greet your children each day. If you are away from them for a few days or even weeks, how do you stay connected?

Sarah: 'I learned to reconnect with my daughter'

When Sarah came to see me she was desperate. She had always enjoyed a warm relationship with her daughter, Anne-Marie, who had just turned thirteen. But something had changed. Anne-Marie would come home late from school, refuse to eat dinner and slam doors, then retreat to her room and spend hours on Snapchat. When Sarah tried to speak to her, Anne-Marie would fold her arms and roll her eyes. Sarah told me, *'I don't know where my little girl's gone.'*

Continued . . .

When Sarah reflected on Anne-Marie's behaviour, she started to recognize that her own anxiety and preoccupation with her new boyfriend had distracted her from giving her daughter the attention and HEART-centred connection she desperately needed.

When Sarah was able to find the calm place within herself and share how she was feeling with Anne-Marie, her daughter surprised her by telling her that she felt bad for letting her down. Sarah, in turn, apologized – providing for her daughter a model of how to admit a mistake. This encouraged Anne-Marie to acknowledge the upset she'd caused to her mother.

By taking time to really listen to one another, they were able to agree to set aside ten to fifteen minutes after school each day when, over a relaxing cup of coffee, Sarah could ask Anne-Marie how her day had gone – if she felt like sharing. The two of them recently spent a Sunday baking together – a sure sign that their connection was getting stronger again.

The art of listening

Though I suffered my share of setbacks when I was growing up, I was fortunate in one crucial respect: my grandmother, Marguerite, was an expert listener. Every evening when she was cooking dinner at our bungalow, she would ask me how my day had gone at school. She always resisted the urge to impose solutions on me when I was struggling, though I now recognize how great the temptation must have been. My grandmother modelled the kind of attentive, non-judgemental listening that I now do my best to explore in my work with parents.

When a child comes to you with a problem – whether it be friends, school or an argument with a sibling – it's natural to want to suggest solutions born of your own much longer life experience. We may instinctively offer advice, perhaps in the way our own parents did when we were upset. Of course, there may be situations where we need to take action as a result of what our child is telling us – particularly if we feel they are at risk in some way. We may even be desperate to ensure our child doesn't repeat mistakes we feel we've made in our lives.

Nevertheless, sometimes we would do better to hold back on the impulse to offer solutions. There will be many times when all your child really wants is someone to empathize with and validate what they're experiencing; they aren't necessarily asking you to make things better or make things go away. Often, the best thing a parent can do is to provide a safe space where their child can be open and honest about how they are feeling. By being there for them in this way, you can help them to learn to face their fears and appreciate the comforting truth that even the most troubling emotions eventually subside, no matter how scary they might seem.

To adult ears, a lot of what preoccupies children can seem trivial – or even boring – compared to 'real' problems. But it's important to remember that the distress a child experiences when worrying is no different to the anxiety we feel as grown-ups. Indeed, if we are too quick to jump in and offer 'fixes', a child may feel that we haven't really understood the depth of the anxiety and hurt they're going through. Equally, when we take time to listen to our child, we may be surprised to discover that they see a situation very differently to us, and that we've made assumptions about what they're thinking without checking whether they are correct. By being good listeners, we provide a role model to help our children develop their own listening skills as well.

You'll have more headspace to focus on your child's concerns if you've been able to find a chance to offload yourself, whether it be with your partner, family or friends. All parents go through crises, including in relationships, health and work, and it's not weak to admit that you need some extra help. Writing down how you are feeling in a journal can also be an immense source of relief – I know first-hand how helpful this can be when you are struggling.

Annie: 'Listening carefully was enough'

'With my kids, I often find myself trying to solve things and find all the answers. But I'm starting to realize the power of just listening, rather than jumping in with a solution.

'The other day, my children were watching a film and they seemed to really be enjoying it. I went through to the kitchen to prepare dinner, and about twenty minutes later my six-year-old son came through in floods of tears. I couldn't work out what was wrong and he said, "The man in the film never got any food." My son got on my knee, and he had to sit and talk about it. Just talking through it, just being empathized with, made him feel much better. Of course, it was only a kids' film, but it was something that in that moment was really important to him. I realized I didn't have to offer any answers. Just being with him and listening carefully was enough.'

Sometimes your child may tell you a story about how they think things unfolded that you know does not correspond to the facts. Remember that this is their perspective on what happened, and it's important to challenge them as respectfully as possible – validating their feelings, if not their interpretation of events. Of course, there is a role for offering solutions or problem-solving. But the act of listening attentively can be a vital first step and much more powerful than any advice we may give. We've all had the experience of wanting to get something off our chest without being judged. Perhaps this act of deep, focused attention will provide an opportunity for your child to reach out for parental guidance, something they may have resisted in the past, or even open a door that will enable them to find a solution for themselves.

On the other hand, you may find yourself in a situation where you feel your child has a legitimate concern but you are truly stumped. That's okay too: children understand that just because you are an adult, it doesn't mean you have all the answers. You're not disappointing them – they can accept that you don't know everything. Being honest with your child is a vital part of a HEART-centred connection because it makes them feel respected. The most important thing is not necessarily coming up with a solution: it's allowing your child to be truly heard.

Like any skill, the art of listening can be honed with practice. Here are some more suggestions for ways to focus on your child as fully as you can:

- **Five deep breaths.** As you start to listen, become aware of your breathing – and take five deep breaths. This will help you to remain centred and present no matter how difficult the conversation gets.

- **Be aware of how you feel in your body.** Keep some attention in your body: notice how your hands feel as they rest in your lap, or the feeling of your feet on the floor. This will help you stay anchored in the here and now.

- **Phone and devices out of the way.** It's obviously important to avoid answering the phone or texting during a conversation – but it's also good to go a step further and ensure the phone is kept out of sight in a bag or pocket and switched into silent mode. Turn off the TV or radio.

- **Active listening.** Reflect back what a child says to you, showing you're empathizing with them and validating their experience. For example, you might say something like, 'So, you're saying you feel sad/frustrated right now?' or 'That must be hard for you.' This is part of an approach called 'active listening' taught by the psychologist Carl Rogers, in which you repeat or paraphrase what you've heard and gently seek clarification if necessary.

- **Avoid interruptions or the temptation to finish another's sentence.** Children can quickly shut down or edit their responses if they don't feel heard. If you do find yourself jumping in – which is normal – take a moment to say you're sorry for interrupting, and go back to active listening.

● **Notice body language – your own as well as your child's.** Ensure your body language is open and friendly, rather than hunched or defensive. You can immediately strike a more receptive pose by uncrossing your arms or legs. If a younger child is on the floor, you might want to get down to their level, or offer a hug or other form of friendly touch if this feels right.

● **Care with words.** Just as we can be more mindful of what our child is saying, so we can choose our own words more carefully. We can pause before responding, notice the effects our words are having and sometimes choose to remain silent if we can't find the right thing to say. Of course, it's natural to feel upset when our child is distressed. It's hard not to get caught up in their anger, sadness or frustration, and before we know it we've said or done something we later regret. But, little by little, it is possible to learn to pause, take a step back and think through your response.

Try It: Really listen

The next time you are talking with your child, see if you can use it as an opportunity to listen more carefully than usual. Offering another person our full attention is one of the most precious gifts we can give:

● Can you sit, for five minutes, just listening, without coming up with a solution?

● Can you bring more focus to the sound of your child's voice, their body language and their facial expression?

● Pay attention to any thoughts and sensations that arise. Do you feel any boredom, irritation or an urge to jump in? Can you observe these feelings and let them pass?

● Can you keep some of your attention on your breath, or in your body?

Afterwards, take a moment to reflect on how it went. Did you feel any difference in the quality of the conversation? How did you feel about yourself when you made a conscious effort to pay attention in this way? How did your child seem to respond? We may find that the act of listening has a more powerful impact on our child than any attempt to try to solve their problems for them.

Naomi: 'I've learned to give advice less and listen more'

'It's so painful to watch my fourteen-year-old daughter, Sophie, struggle with the critical voice in her head. I realize I want to fix things for her because I have exactly the same 'inner critic' myself – she must have inherited it from me. I keep telling her how amazing she is, but she can't seem to hear it. I can see exactly what she needs to do and I want so much to help her because she seems so unhappy and vulnerable. But she never takes any of my advice on board. I keep trying, but nothing I say seems to help.'

I ask Naomi to imagine what kind of feelings would come up for her if she simply listened to Sophie rather than immediately offering advice. Naomi knows she would feel very uncomfortable: even hearing her daughter pouring out her troubles for a few minutes is enough to tie a knot in her stomach. As we discuss this further, Naomi starts to see how her daughter's anxiety triggers a similar anxiety reaction in herself. She remembers all the times in her own life when she's lacked confidence, especially when she was Sophie's age. She realizes that she is a mirror for her daughter's feelings.

As we talk, Naomi starts to reflect on how she interacts with Sophie. She recognizes that she's so anxious to make sure Sophie's okay that she can't resist bombarding her with questions as soon as she gets home from school. Sometimes she catches herself thinking aloud as she tries to understand her daughter, saying things like, 'I think you've got low self-esteem,' or 'I wonder if this is all because your dad's not been around enough?' She does her best to boost her daughter's confidence by telling her how 'amazing' she is and that 'you're beautiful to me'.

Naomi's attempts at reassurance fail to have any impact because Sophie can sense that they are coming from her mum's head, rather than her heart. Sophie simply doesn't feel 'amazing', no matter how many times Naomi tells her how wonderful she is. Sophie doesn't want reassuring *words*; she craves a HEART-centred connection. She wants her mum to show she understands her emotional pain is real, rather than try to talk her out of it because it makes her feel so uncomfortable.

I work with Naomi to remind her to take five deep breaths and remain firmly focused in the present moment whenever she starts to feel anxious. By learning to tolerate her own feelings in this way, she starts to see her anxiety for what it really is: a very unpleasant, yet temporary and fleeting sensation in her stomach. Naomi slowly learns to back off for a

Continued . . .

moment and give her daughter some space. For the first time, she realizes that there is often no need to say much at all. Through her calm and empathic presence, she offers Sophie far more emotional support than any words can convey.

At first, Naomi's own 'inner critic' kicks in and she begins to beat herself up for being such an 'annoying mum' in the past. But as we continue to work together, she recognizes that allowing her own critical voice to run riot in this way isn't helping her or her daughter. Naomi learns to go easier on herself and let her conversations with Sophie unfold with less advice and more pauses. Sophie senses the trust her mum has in her and has gained greater confidence in her ability to find her own answers as a result.

'It's been amazing to see what a difference it makes when I really listen,' Naomi says. 'It's been hard not to rush in with my ideas about what Sophie should or shouldn't do – but the effort's been worth it. I'm focusing now on offering a steady drip-drip of encouragement when things are going well, rather than giving her big chats about how amazing she is. The funny thing is that she has now actually started asking for my opinion rather than always pushing me away. We are definitely more connected than we were, and that feels good.'

Family meetings

In the hectic pace of modern life, it is easy for members of a family to start living separate lives. Our connections start to fray and problems soon follow. Many families I work with find that carving out time in the calendar to hold a 'family meeting' where parents and kids come together at a set time and place is an effective way to keep their connections fresh. Family meetings tend to work best when they are more than just a one-off: everyone makes a commitment to get together on a regular basis, such as every fortnight. However, it's also vital to explain to kids – and particularly teenagers – the goal of the meeting: to create a happier home. It's important to draw a distinction between family meetings and the kind of compulsory commitments teenagers may resist, such as household chores or homework.

You can hold a family meeting for any reason you like, but parents I work with often use them to create a space where adults and children can air any problems that need sorting out, and listen to each other. Some even pass around a 'sharing stick' – perhaps a wooden spoon or small branch from the park or garden – to cut down on interruption and give everyone a chance to talk. The only person allowed to speak is the one holding the stick: everyone else has to listen.

Keep family meetings upbeat and talk about things that have gone well. Taking turns to lead the meetings gives children a chance to feel empowered and validated. It's good to end meetings with something fun, like playing a game. You can post minutes on the fridge to remind everyone of the plans and commitments you made, and always follow through on what you said you would do.

It's also good to set family activity dates on a rotational basis so that everyone gets a chance to choose an activity they enjoy. Set the budget and how far you can travel. Giving your children a chance to play a leadership role in the planning helps them to feel trusted and independent. It also means that if anyone starts whingeing, you can remind them they will have their turn to name the activity another time.

Pets, 'power animals' and imaginary friends

Often one of the first things psychologists do when working with children is to ask them to draw a 'genogram', or family tree. When I was starting out in my career, I would sometimes ask children to include pets, which would go on the diagram in a sibling role. Even in families under the most severe strain, I began to notice that the mere mention of the family cat, dog or hamster would immediately lighten the atmosphere. Over the years, I learned to include this as a routine part of the exercise – and it never fails to make everyone smile.

I have worked with many families where animals have provided a way for children and parents to bond – whether it be through the shared duties of caring for a pet or visiting animals in a sanctuary or urban farm. Animals naturally awaken compassion in children, who can sense they share their own vulnerability. Animals are also the perfect teachers to show us how to live in the moment, not worrying about past or future, happy just to be, exactly as they are.

It's great for any child to have a chance to interact with animals, but for those who are experiencing emotional difficulties of any kind, the experience can be particularly powerful. Children are highly sensitive to how they are perceived by their peers and adults; when looking into the eyes of an animal, they can be sure they are never being judged.

The benefits children can derive from bonding with animals can also extend into the realm of their imaginary friends – whether they be human-like boys or girls, or 'power animals' such as bears, horses or big cats, or even mythical dragons, unicorns or fairies. When I was seven, I met an imaginary lion that helped me during difficult times at school. He would walk ahead of me down the street, offer comforting words and provide a strong, reassuring presence. I could vividly feel his aura of kindness and strength, particularly after I lost my mother.

Younger children don't have to be facing difficulties to invent an imaginary friend, nor is their arrival necessarily a sign that a child is feeling awkward or lonely. In fact, children who have imaginary friends often tend to be particularly creative and empathic. Interacting with imaginary friends can be a great way for them to practise seeing things from different perspectives and develop their imagination, as well as being a wonderful source of humour and fun.

Though we tend to associate imaginary friends with young children, some therapists are discovering that 'power animals' can work well for adults. US psychologist Lisa Schwarz, developer of the Comprehensive Resource Model of psychotherapy, leads her clients in a visualization exercise to meet 'power animals' which help them work through their problems. Schwarz and her colleagues believe that working with 'power animals' in this way may strengthen the pathways in the brain that give us a sense of security and being cared for in our human relationships. As adults, it softens our hearts when we can access the imaginary world and recapture some of the childlike elements of ourselves that we may have forgotten somewhere along the way. If you find that you or your young child is sheltering an invisible house guest, here are some tips:

- Acknowledge the being as a 'real' presence in the household. Be curious about it and try not to dismiss it as a figment of a child's imagination.

- Speaking to the imaginary friend may help you understand your child's perspective on certain issues and strengthen your connection with them.

- Avoid any temptation to speak on behalf of the imaginary friend – this is a relationship 'owned' by the child, and they will have the final say on what this unseen visitor is thinking, feeling or doing.

● Trust your 'inner parent'. It's obviously not acceptable for a child to blame bad behaviour on an imaginary friend, use it as an excuse or follow its 'advice' if it's going to lead them into problems. If conflicts arise, you could use the imaginary friend or 'power animal' to help your child problem-solve. For example, you could ask, 'What would your "friend"/"power animal" do?' to help your child with a particular dilemma. This can be a good way to help them learn to explore new perspectives. No matter what happens, your child will feel empowered if you treat their 'friend' with respect and try to enter into their world.

How to connect with teenagers

Finding ways to spend time with a teenager who's more interested in going to parties or hanging out with groups of friends can be a challenge, but it's important to invest the extra effort: you need to remain their primary emotional support, rather than outsourcing this role to their peers. Other teens can be a great source of camaraderie, but they simply don't have the wisdom, maturity or life experience to provide the guidance your teen will need in every situation. The bond you forge during the teenage years will form the foundation for your relationship as they grow into adulthood, so it's worth persevering as far as you can.

One way of bridging the gap is to welcome their friends into your home, whether it be for a meal, a barbecue or just dropping by at weekends or evenings. This doesn't mean you need to be a 'cool' mum or dad who tries to be one of the gang – teenagers still want parents to be parents. It's more about showing that you respect your teen and are interested in their friends. You obviously can't force your teenager to spend one-on-one time with you, but you can ask them about what they might enjoy doing with you from time to time. Then intentionally carve out a specific time for a shared activity, whether it's a trip to the cinema, a shopping trip, or watching a box set. It's normal for teenagers to yo-yo in their connection with parents: sometimes close, sometimes drifting away. You can signal that the door is always open.

In sensitive teenage years, it's normal for an adolescent to be shy or embarrassed about opening up to their parents. It can be invaluable for a teen to develop a relationship with a 'mentor' figure – perhaps an aunt or uncle, a godparent or other family friend. Teens may feel more comfortable opening up about their problems to somebody slightly removed from their immediate family – and that's not a sign of failure on the part of the parent. As Steve Biddulph, the Australian family therapist, observes: it's often easier to speak to other people's children than our own.

Words matter

It's also worth paying attention to the way you respond to your teenager's troubles. If your teenager begins pouring their heart out, it's tempting to draw on your own experience and say things like, 'I remember what it was like being a teenager – I was one too.' While we are doing our best to understand their perspective, the risk with using these kinds of phrases is that we can inadvertently sound as if we're not really listening. It's a little like the deflation we can feel after confiding in a friend and hearing them say, 'I know how you feel.' Part of us is silently insisting, 'No you don't!' It's the same for teenagers. We all need to feel heard.

As we saw in Step 3, when we feel under pressure we're more likely to slip into the kind of parenting styles we may have inherited from our own parents. We may catch ourselves using phrases we remember from our childhood, or thinking thoughts like these:

- 'She's the child, I'm the adult and she should just do what I say.'

- 'My parents used to shout at me and I turned out okay.'

- 'It's so hard being a parent, I can barely cope.'

- 'All he seems to want to do is play on his computer.'

- 'When I was young I was always out with my friends.'

- Any sentence starting with the phrase, 'Kids now-adays . . .' or 'Typical teenager . . .' should be avoided unless you want an eye-roll in response.

As far as you can, pause before you respond. Take five deep breaths and maintain awareness of your body. Keep some of your attention focused within. However challenging your teen's behaviour may be, the key is to model the kind of qualities you'd like to see them display – even if they may test you mightily in the process. Try to suspend judgement. I am often struck by how much teenagers fear disappointing their parents, no matter how nonchalant they may appear. Deep down, many are concerned by the amount of distress and worry they may be causing and will often readily respond if you choose to extend an olive branch.

Setting aside your mask

Children tend to be highly perceptive, but teens have a laser-like ability to see through a lack of authenticity in any form. No matter what you say, they will notice how you are *being* – with other people, and in your relationship with your partner. They will be acutely aware of how much compassion you show to others, and particularly to yourself. It may not always seem like it, but they can also sense very clearly when adults like, respect and trust them – and are able to see them as a unique individual, regardless of how they may be behaving in that moment. Above all, in caring for your teen, try to remember to be kind to yourself. There will inevitably be times when you react to challenges in ways you might later regret. That's okay, and part of what it means to be a parent. Each moment is a new moment, and each day an opportunity to start again.

How conflict can bring us closer

Rows, tears, angry words and slammed doors are an inevitable part of any parent–child relationship, but the hurt feelings they cause can linger. As adults, our instinct may be to put the upset behind us as quickly as possible and move on, secure in the knowledge that we've weathered many such storms in the past without any lasting harm. Or we might even feel guilty if we lost our temper or used harsh words and prefer to pretend the whole episode never happened. We may assume that our child's silence means that all has been forgiven. Children and teens don't have the benefit of our experience, however, and their hurt feelings may feel to them as though they will never go away, or their resentment towards us may last longer than we might assume.

As adults, it's up to us to take the lead in repairing these cracks to ensure they don't lead to bigger problems. Everyday tensions and disagreements can build up over time, leading to ever more frequent misunderstandings and pointed fingers. We may be justifiably angry, and feel disrespected by children who seem to be walking all over us or taking us for granted. But by finding the humility to revisit what happened when we're feeling calmer, we can turn the aftermath of conflicts into opportunities to deepen our connection. All relationships need work, and taking these moments to make sure that any outstanding grievance has been aired and resolved is one of the most powerful ways we can strengthen our family's foundations.

The power of laughter

Parenting can feel very serious at times, so it's good to allow yourself the odd moment to reconnect with your own light-heartedness and laughter. Becoming more present can help us to rediscover some of the qualities of curiosity, playfulness and imagination that come so naturally to young people but which can easily be overtaken by our commitments as parents. Don't underestimate what every child knows: the power of humour to cut through an argument and lift a heavy atmosphere. We can't be anywhere else than in the moment if we're laughing. Possibilities might include:

- Rough-and-tumble play

- Watching funny videos on YouTube

- Feeding ducks at the local river or pond

- Collecting leaves, acorns or conkers in a park

- Dancing to fun tunes

- Going barefoot
- Dressing-up
- Playing charades or another family game
- Putting on a silly voice

The five key points

Connect with your child every day

- Your relationship with your child is the foundation for everything: make connecting a priority.

- Whenever you run into 'bad' behaviour, ask yourself: 'Does my child feel connected to me?'

- You don't need all the answers as a parent: sometimes just listening is enough.

- Family meetings can be a great way to strengthen your bond.

- Don't forget to laugh.

Set limits to help your kids feel safe

Mums and dads often find it hard to tell their children 'no'. But making clear what behaviour is and isn't acceptable is one of our most important jobs. Clear and consistent rules make kids feel safe. Setting limits – and sticking to them – is a sign you love your children.

As any parent knows, children are wired to test boundaries – it's an important part of growing up and learning how the world works. They may get upset, frustrated, angry and disappointed when they don't get their own way. But they will feel much more secure in the long run if they know that there is a confident adult in charge who knows right from wrong.

As your children get older, there's no easy way to strike

a balance between the need to give them more independence and the importance of setting boundaries that feel right for you. Of course you want to protect your children, but on the other hand older children and teens won't benefit from being micro-managed or feeling that you don't trust them. Take it one step at a time. See how they respond to a certain degree of increased responsibility and let them show you how they get on. Ask your 'inner parent': are they ready to handle a little bit more freedom, or have you given them more than they can currently cope with? Children will only be able to develop their competencies if you set your expectations on the high side – and they have to be allowed to make a few mistakes along the way.

How to set limits with your children

Here are some tips for deciding on boundaries and sticking to them:

- **Be clear with yourself ahead of time.** Whether dealing with a child who refuses to brush their teeth or a teen who is always in trouble, decide before a confrontation what your limits will be.

- **Involve your children in the boundary setting where possible and appropriate.** When children share ownership of rules they are more invested in sticking to them.

- **Choose your battles.** Think about what really matters to you. Pour more energy into maintaining the boundaries that matter most: it won't matter too much if you relax a little on minor rules on days when you feel tired, fed up or stressed.

- **Take charge and be confident in your decisions.** Children want to be led – so be a leader.

- **If you have a partner, support each other.** It's much easier if you can manage to work as a team. Don't undermine each other by playing good cop/bad cop.

- **Set clear consequences.** Children learn better when they know that crossing a certain line will result in a specific negative consequence. With teenagers, it is better to let them experience the natural consequences of their actions as far as you can, while still keeping them safe.

- **Be consistent.** Children are much more likely to follow rules that are consistently applied.

- **Don't make threats.** If you threaten a child with a certain consequence in the heat of the moment, then don't follow through, they will respect you less. Best to wait until things have calmed down. You can then decide on what actions to take – and clearly explain to your child what they have done to trigger them.

- **Don't explain the reason for a limit more than once.** It's good to explain why you have created a rule but you will appear weak if you keep repeating yourself.

- **See things from your child's point of view.** Imposing limits doesn't mean we stop empathizing with our child. We can make an effort to understand why they are feeling so angry, disappointed and upset without compromising on the boundaries we've put in place.

No means no

Children will often come up with ways to try to make you change your mind, including begging or going on and on in the hope you will eventually come round. Don't compromise. If you give in once, your children will learn that they can wear you down if they try hard enough. The next time they want something, you won't hear the end of it until you give in again. Ignore the begging from the start, and if they persist, you can tell them kindly but firmly that you have made up your mind and won't be talking any further about the subject. If you stand firm, they will soon realize that moaning is a waste of time.

By saying 'no' to your child, you are teaching them crucial life skills. If they don't ever hear you say 'no', they will find it difficult to say 'no' to others and set their own boundaries in adulthood.

Why setting boundaries can be so hard

Telling a child what they can and can't do is one of the trickiest parts of any parent's job. So many mums and dads tell me they find it difficult to know where to place boundaries and how to teach their child right from wrong. Everyone can agree that learning to accept the feeling of frustration and disappointment of not getting what you want is an essential part of growing up. It's easy to forget that parents face their own equivalent of this process: learning to work with their own hurt feelings, frustrations and confusion in the face of their child's hostility, rejection or anger. When confronted with a child who is pushing limits, it's easy to be pulled in several directions at once:

- **Our own parental influences.** We can find ourselves automatically resorting to the kind of discipline strategies our own parents may have used on us, regardless of whether they fit with our values or what our 'inner parent' would choose.

- **Voices of our partner, friends or relatives.** We defer to the many people telling us how to parent – with their advice often reflecting the influence of their own parents.

- **Feeling our child's distress.** Our child's upset can reawaken the part within all of us that remembers how we felt as children when we didn't get our own way, or felt our needs were not being met.

The first step towards becoming more comfortable with setting limits is to acknowledge how difficult it can be. The more you can become aware of the competing influences, the more you can step back and take the pause needed to listen to the voice of your 'inner parent' and choose your response in any given moment. There is no fixed answer or universal strategy that will work for all children at all times. You will be in a much better position to know what the situation requires if you're able to take five deep breaths and trust your own judgement.

It helps to remember that children need structure. Some mums and dads fear their child will misinterpret their firmness as a sign of coldness or lack of love. I reassure them that this fear is misplaced: as long as our boundaries spring from a kind and open heart, they will do no harm. Setting limits is not about power and control – it's a vital part of the kind of HEART-centred connection we spoke about in the introduction. Kids love confident parents who show leadership, as well as compassion and empathy. They will respond well when you take the time to explain clearly the reasons why you have decided on certain limits, and that you want to work with them to keep them safe.

Even when a child does not understand the reason for a boundary, they will feel more confident when they discover their parents draw clear, consistent lines, no matter how much they might complain and cry, 'It's not *fair*!' It becomes easier to stand our ground when we recognize that a child's attempts to push boundaries are their way of exploring how the world works – and frequently a bid for our attention, even if delivered clumsily and in a way that's more likely to provoke our irritation than our affection.

How you go about setting limits will vary according to the temperament of your child and the way they develop as they get older. If a young child complains and manipulates you to win a reprieve, they may appear momentarily satisfied – but in reality the feeling of being stronger than their parent will make them feel very uneasy. However much they may whine and complain, and say, 'You never let me have my way,' or 'I never get what I want,' a child will respect you if you stick to your word.

We all want our children to like us, but ultimately our role is not to be their friend, but to be their parent. Children can only feel fully secure when they know where the boundaries lie. Setting rules with clear consequences for breaking them is not about being a dictator: it's an act of love that helps our children learn to navigate the rule-based world outside their home.

Getting your children to listen

Getting your children to listen and follow instructions can sometimes seem like an impossible task. So many mums and dads tell me that their kids seem to have selective hearing and will not comply with simple requests such as brushing their teeth or leaving the house on time. It's easy to end up feeling so exasperated that you start shouting and then feel like a failure for losing your temper. Children can learn to tune us out and only start to pay attention when we have started screaming at them.

The change must begin with us as parents. We need to look at ourselves and become more aware of how we respond when our children seem to ignore us. It's incredibly frustrating, but we must resist the temptation to interpret their behaviour as a sign of rejection or that we have failed as parents in some way. If you are not happy with how your child is responding, then it's up to you to take charge and create a different situation where you feel more in control.

We talked in Step 4 about how to listen to your child. Here are some tips for getting your child to listen to you:

- **Choose your moment.** A child is more likely to take what you say on board if they are feeling relaxed. It may be better to wait rather than broach a difficult topic first thing in the morning or straight after a busy school day.

- **Get your child's full attention.** Get down to their eye level so that you can make eye contact.

- **Minimize distractions.** Turn off the television, put your phone away and ask your child to put down games or phones.

- **Be in close proximity to your child.** Try and be in the same room rather than shouting from another room.

• **Be aware of your voice.** Speak in calm, warm, even tones.

• **Take responsibility for your own feelings.** Describe how you feel when they don't listen. Explain how happy you would be if you didn't have to repeat yourself.

• **Use simple, clear instructions.** Be clear, brief and to the point. Adele Faber and Elaine Mazlish, family therapists, advise that sometimes you can offer reminders in a single word, such as 'teeth' if you want them to brush their teeth.

• **Be firm.** Tell your children what to do, don't ask. Unless you want to offer a choice, avoid phrasing instructions in the form of questions such as 'would you', 'can you', 'could you', 'should we' and 'shall we'. Don't throw an 'okay?' at the end of your instruction since it's an invitation for your child to say 'no'.

• **Give instructions one at a time.** If you have a list of things for your child to do, make sure they know the order they need to do them in.

• **Pause.** After giving a set of instructions, pause for a few seconds to allow your child to process the information. Research has shown that kids are more likely to follow directions if you give them a chance to think in this way.

- **Check they have understood.** Ask your child to repeat your instruction back to you.

- **Use when/then phrasing.** Make it clear what benefit your child can expect in return for complying, such as: 'When you've brushed your teeth, then I'll read you a story.'

- **Explain the logic behind your instructions.** All of us rebel against being told what to do if we feel we're being nagged. Children are more likely to respond if they know why they are being given a certain instruction. For example: 'we turn the lights off because it saves electricity.'

- **Use visual cues.** Signs or timetables can be helpful to remind kids of their routine and what they have agreed to do.

- **Be age appropriate.** Use simpler words to speak to younger children, and be clear with older ones without being patronizing. Children old enough to read may respond well to notes, which may help them feel more grown up.

- **Use five-minute warnings.** Children may fall into line more readily if you give them a warning shortly before a boundary is about to come into force. For example: 'In five minutes it will be time to get off the computer and sit down at the table for dinner.'

- **Manage transitions.** Let children, particularly younger ones, know plans ahead of time. For example: 'After you have brushed your teeth, you can watch a little more television before we go out to see Grandma.'

- **Praise and reward cooperation.** Show that you appreciate their good listening skills.

Naughtiness or bid for attention?

Children can be at their most exasperating when they seem deliberately to act up or misbehave for no apparent reason. It can be very easy for a despairing parent confronted with a boundary-pushing child to slip into self-blame and wonder if they're doing the right thing. In our frustration, we may even start to think of our child as 'ungrateful', 'difficult' or 'selfish'. However much we may want to, it's not always easy to see our child from the fresh perspective of somebody who is meeting them for the first time.

It's also important to recognize that there will be times when your child is so hard to cope with that you may experience strong feelings of resentment towards them. Many parents I see tell me they feel bad when this happens. I always tell them to go a little easier on themselves. A surge of resentment does not mean you don't love your child – every parent struggles with this and it's normal to go through moments when you just don't like them very much. It's important in these situations to draw a distinction between the child you love and the behaviour you don't like. Try to take a step back and consider what may lie beneath your child's behaviour, rather than focusing on what they are doing wrong.

When your child is trying to get your attention, it's often a bid for a deeper connection – whether they are being 'good' or 'bad'. What can seem like acting up or naughtiness can be a misguided attempt to form the HEART-centred connection they crave. Of course, many factors can drive challenging behaviour, from tiredness and hunger to a bad day at school or tension with a sibling. However, when confronted with a persistent pattern, it may be worth asking whether it's your child's way of saying:

- 'I want you to listen to me.'

- 'I want your attention.'

- 'I want to feel like I'm a worthy person.'

- 'I want to know you love me.'

- 'I want to know that I can trust you to be my place of safety.'

- 'I want some of your time – just you and me, no distractions.'

Rather than reacting immediately, the first step you can take towards defusing the situation is to notice whether your child's behaviour has triggered a spike in your own feelings of anger, frustration or self-blame. This is the moment to take a pause and ask your 'inner parent' what is the right thing to do. There will be time later to address the deeper issues – but it's obviously counter-productive to react in the heat of the moment. It may be that you need to hug your child, leave the room for a short while, or drop down to their level and quietly speak to them. If they're older, it might be time to recognize that you're both getting stressed and press the pause button by asking, 'Do we both need to take a few minutes before we speak again?'

Responding to rejection

Rejection of any kind can be painful, but being rejected by your own child can seem unbearable. All of us have 'rejection buttons' that can be pushed when a relatively trivial experience of rejection in the present brings up much rawer feelings from our past. This is likely to happen more often as your child enters the teenage years, when they will naturally want to assert their independence and test what happens when they defy you.

It may help to reflect on the fact that an angry child is not actually rejecting you; on the contrary, they are projecting their emotional turmoil on to you precisely because they need you. Your job is to see their reaction for what it is: their way to express overwhelming feelings they have not yet learned to manage. It's exhausting to deal with a difficult child or teen on a daily basis, and sometimes you might feel as if you've simply had enough. But by learning to see *through* their drama, you can take it less personally. The one thing you can always do is take responsibility for your own feelings and try to stay as calm and centred as you can.

Indeed, the very moments when children or teenagers are pushing you away or withdrawing are the times they need you to remain the 'safe haven' to which they will eventually return. As long as you are able to hold a steady space within yourself, they will sense it at some deep level – even if they have just stormed out of the room or refused to eat the dinner you so carefully prepared. As the parent, you have greater self-awareness, and the ability to pause and choose whether to perpetuate the cycle of acting out past hurts, or create a space for something new to take their place.

Allowing tears to flow

If we're facing daily battles with our children over discipline, we need to remember that our bodies are designed to cry. We can probably all recall a time from childhood when allowing ourselves to surrender to our urge to sob brought a profound feeling of relief. There are very real, physiological reasons why letting go in this way can be so healthy. Researchers have discovered that crying tears of sadness helps wash many types of stress hormones out of the system and causes the body to release a natural pain-killer called leucine enkephalin.

Yet for all the healing balm that crying offers, adults often struggle to connect to their tears. The US family therapist Susan Stiffelman says she often sees people with what she calls 'dry-eyed syndrome': no matter how intense their sadness or grief, they simply cannot start releasing these feelings by crying. In my experience, the same is often true in Britain. I've had so many parents from all walks of life say to me, 'I know the tears are there, but I just cannot cry.' There often seems to be a fear of the temporary loss of control that tears may bring. We've convinced ourselves that we're fine as long as we're not crying – when crying is the very thing that could make us feel better. One mother said, 'I know I need to cry, but I'm afraid once I start I'll never stop.'

Our resistance to crying can colour our response to the tears of others. How many of us feel uncomfortable when a friend starts to sob and immediately rush in to try to cheer them up? Of course, helping somebody work through their problems is often the right thing to do. But when tears are in full flow, it can be even more powerful to resist the impulse to offer reassurance and meet another's sorrow or grief with silent companionship. Far from being a sign of weakness, having the courage to face these feelings – however many tears they evoke – is a mark of strength.

Our tears can also provide a powerful opportunity to deepen our HEART-centred connection with our child.

Children, particularly when they are younger, are acutely aware of how they are perceived by their parents and will do almost anything to please them, including squashing their urge to cry. One thirteen-year-old girl would always hold back from the brink of tears, saying, 'I'm all right, I'm all right. My mum wants me to be okay, she doesn't want me to be upset or see me crying.' She is far from alone. Young boys also need mature masculine role models who can show them that it's not a sign of weakness to show they are sad sometimes. Some kids will lash out in anger precisely because expressing aggression feels safer to them than revealing their vulnerability through tears.

Learning to forgive our child – and ourselves

However much we may try, it's not always easy to maintain a HEART-centred connection with our child: life has a habit of getting in the way. We can all lose our temper in a way we later regret, and we can all find ourselves giving in to a child's relentless demands at the end of a long day of doing our utmost to maintain firm boundaries. That's why cultivating forgiveness is so important – both for yourself and for your child.

The 'frenemy' in our head is often very reluctant to let us forgive ourselves. But we can perhaps find a moment to show ourselves some compassion. Ask if you can forgive yourself for:

- Losing my temper

- Not saying the right thing

- Resenting my child

- Feeling like a failure

- Comparing myself unfavourably to others

One friend of mine who looks after her children full-time said that at times it can be a lonely and thankless task being a parent; she has accepted that her husband, her own parents and her children will probably never express the kind of appreciation that deep down she would love. Instead, she tries as often as she can to tell herself, 'You're doing really well.' She has recognized and accepted the need to be her own cheerleader. If I were to be granted ten seconds to offer one message to each of the mums and dads I work with, it would be this: even the smallest steps you can take towards being kinder to yourself matter far more than you might imagine.

The five key points

Set limits to help your kids feel safe

- Setting boundaries can be hard, but they make kids feel safe.

- Even when they play up, deep down our children want us to be their leaders.

- Learn to say no.

- We all have rejection buttons: try to take your kids' behaviour less personally.

- Parenting is messy: learn to forgive yourself and your child.

Allow your child some bumps

In my work, I see countless young people who lack any confidence in their ability to pick themselves up from a fall. They are paralysed by a fear of trying new things in case they make a mistake. They feel they can't cope, they worry about the future and they're scared of letting their parents down. The many pressures these young people face – from mounting academic demands to the uncertainties of gaining access to higher education, jobs and homes – are very real. But it's these very pressures that make it more important than ever that our children acquire the resilience they need to navigate the challenges of adolescence and adulthood. They can only do this if they are allowed to make mistakes and fail sometimes.

This can be a difficult process for parents to watch.

Mums and dads tell me they are often taken aback by the intensity of the protective instinct that kicked in when they had children. This is only natural: the overwhelming urge to protect our young is a product of millions of years of evolution – it's what's kept the human race going. We all know that falling and picking yourself up again is an essential part of growing up, but the 'parent alarm' can be so sensitive that it can make it extremely hard to watch your child struggle, even for a moment. How do we get the balance right? There are no fixed answers, but allowing a child to overcome challenges in a safe, contained way is essential to help them build their confidence and their life skills – and it sends a powerful message that you trust them.

Whether it's tripping over in the playground, working through conflicts with friends or coping with the death of a much-loved pet, the experience of overcoming adversity is essential to shaping a child's fast-developing brain. As the Canadian psychologist Gordon Neufeld argues, kids *need* sometimes to experience setbacks, sadness and disappointment, otherwise they won't learn to cope with their vulnerable feelings and they will find it difficult to function as independent adults.

Watching your child struggle is never easy. The key is to observe yourself closely and with curiosity to see what comes up for you when your son or daughter is having a hard time. Perhaps you feel a sense of failure and disappointment if your child didn't get the test results they wanted. You may feel angry if your teenager has been caught cyber-bullying another child. Or you may feel an intense sadness when your daughter's friends are giving her the silent treatment. It's no wonder we're often tempted to wade in on their behalf.

Nevertheless, the more you can resist the impulse to react immediately to your own difficult feelings, the more you will be able to soothe your child's temporary distress. Creating a space where you can allow your child to be angry, sad or frustrated and then help them figure out what action to take for themselves is far more valuable than rushing in to try to fix everything for them. Of course, there are times when it is necessary to intervene to keep a child safe – but kids are a lot tougher than we think. There is a core of resilience in every young person – but they can only unearth it and learn to trust themselves if they are sometimes allowed to face disappointment, boredom or not getting what they want. Consult your 'inner parent': perhaps what seems like a setback for your child is actually a great opportunity for them to learn and grow.

Cultivating a 'growth mindset'

In the 1990s, the conventional wisdom among psychologists in the 'self-esteem movement' was that the best thing parents could do to help their children was to reinforce their positive self-image by telling them how clever, talented or artistic they were. More recent research suggests that this approach can backfire because children can internalize a fixed idea of themselves that can leave them more vulnerable when things don't turn out the way they had hoped. Children who are constantly told that they are super-intelligent or better than others can become so paralysed by a fear of failure that they struggle to get started or complete tasks. There's a world of difference between a healthy commitment to high standards and the kind of relentless perfectionism that means children put themselves under so much pressure that they can't cope when they achieve anything less than an A*. Children whose self-worth is dependent on success and achievement often live with a harsh 'inner critic' that deters them from trying new things. We can all help our children learn to become more confident if we start to redefine our own idea of success. Rather than focusing purely on external markers of achievement, perhaps we can think more in terms of the unique contribution we can each make to the world and each other.

We need to help young people move away from all-or-nothing thinking and look at situations more flexibly. Our children will be far better equipped to cope with life's untidy realities if they can say to themselves, 'I'd *like* to do well at English' rather than 'I *must* get an A* and anything less would be a disaster'. They can then learn to see 'mistakes' or 'failures' as opportunities to learn and grow rather than as evidence of some inherent flaw that needs to be corrected. Young people will value themselves more if we focus on praising the effort they make rather than the end result. With this in mind, you might wish to use these kinds of phrases when encouraging your children:

- 'I can see that you're trying hard.'

- 'I know it didn't work out this time, but the main thing is the effort you made.'

- 'I admire the way you [add example of something your child does well].'

Psychologists have demonstrated the benefits of this approach. Professor Carol Dweck and fellow researchers at Stanford University have found that students praised for their intelligence tended to choose easier tasks within their comfort zone, apparently fearing the consequences of failure. Those praised for their effort, by contrast, chose to work on problems that would stretch their abilities. The researchers described the two approaches in terms of 'mindsets':

- **Fixed mindset.** Kids who were constantly told they were smart or successful viewed intelligence as a fixed quantity that they either did or didn't possess. They worried about *proving* their ability rather than improving, and were less likely to take on difficult problems and more likely to get upset if they failed.

- **Growth mindset.** Kids who were taught that intelligence is a malleable quality that can be increased

with effort and learning tended to have more constructive thoughts and were more flexible about
changing their strategy if what they were doing wasn't
working.

These differences were reflected in brain activity. For example,
after being given the solution to a test question they
had answered incorrectly, students with a 'growth mindset'
displayed greater activation of brain regions associated
with the deep processing of language – suggesting that
they were confronting their mistake and trying to learn
from it. Indeed, activation in this brain region predicted
better performance in a later test.

The way you give praise can help to cultivate a 'growth
mindset'. For example, when a child seeking approval
shows you a piece of work, look for specific details to praise,
rather than making generalizations about how talented
they are. For example, 'I love the colours in this picture'
rather than 'You're such a great artist.'

Another sure way to help your child cultivate a 'growth
mindset' is to help them spend as much time as possible
outdoors. Exploring nature, with all its rugged obstacles, is
an excellent way to provide them with opportunities to
learn to assess risk and problem-solve for themselves.

Ayesha: 'They're learning valuable lessons'

'My ten-year-old, Arshad, was saying, "I'm bored!" I screamed, "You can just be bored then!" I felt bad. I felt like I should be trying to make everything okay for him. But I can't. I'm so tired and I feel like I'm at my limit. But you just want to make it all all right for them, don't you? You want to make everything okay.

'Later, in the playground, I saw another boy being mean to my son. All these strong emotions came to the surface, and I felt a surge of anger towards that other child. I wanted to throttle him. That instinct to protect my child is so strong that I could never have imagined how difficult it would be to override those angry feelings and not react immediately.

'But I know the reality is that I'm not doing Arshad any favours in the long term. The reality is that my son will have to learn to manage his own friendships and be disappointed sometimes – even though I'm his greatest supporter, and I'll always be there for him. And sometimes he'll just have to learn to amuse himself like we used to – I can't constantly keep coming up with new, exciting things for him to do. He needs to learn that there can't always be an adult to entertain him, and that he'll still be okay.'

Be honest with yourself: Are you putting your emotional needs before the good of your kids?

As parents, we need to allow our children to explore the world and maybe suffer some bumps along the way – it's the only way they can develop healthy self-confidence. We know this deep down, but so many of us hover over our kids like 'helicopters', ready to rush in to help at the first sign of distress. Why?

If you lack confidence in yourself, parenting can bring up intense feelings of anxiety. Understandably, you may feel an almost overwhelming urge to hover over your child. You may tell yourself you only want to protect them, but in reality you are playing 'helicopter' to try to escape your own anxieties about being a parent. Or perhaps you are overcompensating for what was missing in your own childhood, if one or both of your parents were absent, whether physically or emotionally. You may feel that you were not given the care and attention you needed and you want to make sure your own children feel the sense of protection and safety you never had.

Others worry about their children's future and want to ensure they have done everything possible to give them the best chance of success. Although such parents may tell themselves they need to hover so they can seize every opportunity to help their child get ahead, sometimes these parents are not being entirely honest with themselves: they may be feeding their own insecurities at the expense of their child's need to develop independence and resilience.

Some parents live their lives through their children to such a degree that they feel their child's failures and successes as acutely as if they were their own. While it's natural to wish the best for your child, this kind of 'over-parenting' can make a child feel enormously pressured and undermine their relationship with their parents in the long term. Some children I have worked with are so aware of how much time and money their parents have invested in them that they have become completely paralysed by a fear of failure. They worry that they will let their parents down.

If you recognize yourself in any of the above, can you take a deep breath and look squarely at what is really driving you? Perhaps you fear being a bad parent, or you fear your child will not achieve the success you so desperately want for them. The more awareness you can bring to your fears, the more you can begin to take a pause, and ask yourself whether you want to let anxiety dictate your parenting style, or whether you could live more in alignment with your values. Look inside yourself: are high grades and a well-paid job in the system really as important as resilience, creativity and compassion?

Sometimes we have to let our children face the consequences of their actions. It may go against all of your protective instincts, but remember you don't always have to fix everything for your children. If they have forgotten their PE kit or homework, sometimes it is okay for them to face the music: it's the only way they will learn the lesson and remember for next time. Making mistakes and learning to fail well are important life skills: we must not deprive our children of these vital lessons.

As in all aspects of parenting, self-awareness is the key. Be honest with yourself about whether your parenting choices are based on a clear evaluation of what is best for your child, or whether they are driven by your own unresolved emotions. Parents must learn that their children are separate individuals, not extensions of themselves. Children need to learn to cope with setbacks and disappointment if they are going to learn to function independently in the adult world. None of this is easy: all of us have blind spots as parents. So remember to go easy on yourself and forgive yourself as you learn.

Managing Sibling Rivalry

Every child wants to feel special, so the presence of a sibling can often cause feelings of jealousy or resentment. It can be frustrating and upsetting as parents to watch our kids compete with each other for our attention. Here are some tips for keeping the peace:

- **Only intervene when necessary.** Try not to get involved in minor squabbles. Better to let them work it out for themselves if they can, and learn how to resolve their differences. You will obviously have to step in if they can't stop arguing or things get too aggressive.

- **Stay neutral.** Taking sides will only make the situation worse, and create further tension.

- **Allow everyone to calm down and then listen.** Let your kids speak one at a time without being interrupted so they can share their version of what happened.

- **Problem solve.** Guide your children to find a solution that works for everyone and help them develop the skills they will need to handle future conflicts more skilfully.

- **Remember that every child is unique.** Focus on meeting their individual needs. Some may need more one-on-one time, others may want more help managing their emotions. Make sure all your children know they will always be loved.

Boys also cry

Until recently, many men in our society felt like they didn't have permission to express their sadness or grief, and have lacked male role models capable of showing them how. If we don't start teaching our sons that it's okay to cry, men will continue to bottle up their feelings and never learn to deal with their emotions in a healthy, mature way. This can have devastating, long-term effects on their mental health, relationships and ability to connect emotionally to others.

Here are my top tips for helping your son to learn that it's okay to cry:

● **Explain that crying is healthy.** Boys need to know that tears are a natural response that help to release stress, not something to feel ashamed about.

● **Lead by example.** How comfortable do you feel with crying? What messages were you given about expressing your emotions when you were growing up? Were you ever told by the adults around you to 'Stop crying', or 'Don't be sad', or 'Be brave'? So many of us have been conditioned by our culture not to cry that we struggle to connect to our tears. If we want to raise emotionally healthy sons we need to demonstrate that we can handle our own challenging feelings. After all, our children learn more by what we do than what we say. So let your sons see you cry and show them that it's a normal reaction. Show that having the courage to face all of our feelings, however many tears they evoke, is a mark of real strength.

● **Make space to listen.** Create a safe home environment where your son can be open and honest. Let him know that you are always there to listen and will never judge him. Resist the urge to offer solutions. There will be many times when all your son really wants is someone to empathize with and validate what he's experiencing: he is not necessarily asking you to make all his problems go away. By being there for your son in this way, you can help him to learn to face his feelings and understand that even the most troubling emotions eventually subside, no matter how scary they might seem.

● **Provide tools to manage big feelings.** Be aware that some boys will lash out in anger precisely because expressing aggression feels safer and more acceptable to them than revealing their vulnerability

Continued . . .

through tears. So give him the tools to manage his anger and other overwhelming feelings, for example by taking a ten-minute break to calm down or run around the block to let off steam. Teach your son that he does not need to do the tough boy act in the playground and that there are alternative, respectful ways of dealing with conflict.

● **Nurture relationships with positive male role models.** Even if your son doesn't have a father present in his life, it can be invaluable for him to develop a relationship with a 'mentor' figure – perhaps an uncle, cousin, grandfather, stepdad, godparent or other family friend. Young boys need mature masculine role models who can demonstrate to them that it's not a sign of weakness to show they are sad sometimes. Such men can show them that it's okay to feel vulnerbale or sensitive, or to act with compassion, and that they will still be accepted by other men.

● **Question what it means to be a man.** We've all heard the expressions 'Big boys don't cry', 'Stop crying like a girl', 'Be a man', and 'Man up'. We can't control the messages that society sends our sons about masculinity, but we can be mindful about the way we speak to them. So discuss what being a man really means and challenge the stereotypical ideas that 'real' men don't express their emotions. Show your son that being a man is not about succumbing to peer pressure and that he doesn't need the approval of aggressive men. Be open to new definitions of masculinity and learn to see your son as a unique individual who will express masculinity in his own way. Help him learn to trust his own judgement and respect himself and others, particularly in the way he relates to women.

The five key points

Allow your child some bumps

- Allow your child some bumps: it's the only way to build resilience.

- Help your kids develop a 'growth mindset'.

- Notice when your own anxiety is causing you to be over-protective of your child.

- Sometimes it's good to let kids face the consequences of their actions.

- Resist the urge to problem-solve: help your child figure out answers for themselves.

Step 7

Teach your child about their brain

It's a scene that so many parents have learned to dread: your child's face scrunches, tears well and the scream begins – a piercing, nerve-shredding wail that just won't seem to stop. The feeling triggers a reaction in your own body: your heart sinks, your jaw tightens and frustration starts to build. You're already late, but no matter how much you try to cajole, reason with or comfort your child, nothing seems to work. Your own anger begins to simmer in response. 'I hate you so much,' your child shouts – and suddenly you're filled with a feeling of profound hostility towards the very person you love the most.

There can be few greater challenges to maintaining

your inner balance than a child's full-blown meltdown. Temper tantrums are one of the most common – and most difficult – problems parents face, often leaving us with a feeling that we cannot 'find our child' underneath all the rage and tears. It's no wonder we can quickly reach boiling point ourselves and end up acting in ways we may later regret. It can be very easy to take our child's behaviour personally and start telling ourselves that their moods must be a reflection of our poor parenting skills. Many of the parents I've seen have relentlessly beaten themselves up because they feel they should be able to manage their children's tantrums without ending up so shouty and stressed. The fact that every mum and dad feels helpless sometimes doesn't make it any easier.

These are the kinds of things I often hear from parents:

- 'Not being able to fix my child's anger makes me feel powerless.'

- 'I feel like strangers are judging me when my child acts up in public.'

- 'I feel embarrassed that I can't seem to control my child.'

- 'If we don't sort this out quickly, the teenage years are going to be even worse.'

- 'I can't understand why she lashes out at the people who love her.'

- 'It's painful to hear someone I love so much being so disrespectful.'

- 'I'm scared of my child when he gets angry.'

- 'I feel so guilty that somehow I did something wrong in the early years, and now he hates me, and all I want is for him to love me.'

I find that it can be hugely helpful to consider your child's behaviour from a new perspective: the fast-developing field of neuroscience. Though we may belong to a more stressed-out generation than our parents, we also have one big advantage: advances in neuro-imaging mean we know a lot more about how a child's brain develops in their early years. Parents may be quick to blame themselves, but emotional storms gripping a child are often less a symptom of some parental failing than they are the result of a temporary mismatch between the thinking and feeling parts of a young brain. Children have a lot of energy – and that's a wonderful blessing. In this step we look at how to channel this energy in the healthiest possible ways using what we know about how their brains work – and to empower our kids by teaching them some of this knowledge in appropriate ways.

How your child's brain develops

We can all see the very obvious outer changes that occur as a child grows up, but the most important developments happen on the inside. Human brains are comprised of about eighty-six billion neurons – specialized nerve cells that relay information throughout the brain and nervous system. Babies are born with almost all the neurons they will ever have already in place, but the brain itself grows rapidly, doubling in size in the first year and reaching 80 per cent of its adult volume by the age of three.

As recently as twenty years ago, it was thought that brain development stopped in early childhood. Neuroscientists have since discovered that further phases of major development take place until the age of about twelve, and then again in the teenage years. The adolescent brain undergoes extensive remodelling as teens refine their communication, learning and social skills. Some experts believe these changes help explain why teenagers can be so impulsive and difficult to handle: their brains aren't fully developed until they reach the age of twenty-five.

A number of pioneering researchers have sought to harness what they've learned about young brains to provide practical advice for parents helping children gradually learn to regulate their emotions and think more clearly. One of the leaders in this field is the American neuropsychiatrist Dr Daniel Siegel. In his book *The Whole-Brain Child*, co-authored with Dr Tina Payne Bryson, he provides a simplified portrait of the brain as being divided into two halves – a little like the floors of a two-storey house:

- **Downstairs brain.** This is the primitive part of the brain that controls all the things newborn babies can do – breathing, eating, sleeping, blinking and so on. The 'downstairs' brain is where our emotions happen. It also houses the amygdala – a tiny, almond-shaped component that serves as the brain's 'smoke alarm' – and is constantly scanning for danger.

- **Upstairs brain.** Think of a light-filled study lined with books. Also known as the 'prefrontal cortex', this part of the brain allows us to think clearly, plan for the future, make decisions, solve problems, use language and empathize with others. This part of the brain has a kind of 'neural wi-fi' that allows us to understand what others are feeling and respond appropriately. The prefrontal cortex is fully developed only when a child reaches early adulthood.

- **The stairway.** In adults, there is a kind of metaphorical 'stairway' linking the 'upstairs' brain and the 'downstairs' brain, with chemical messengers constantly relaying information between the floors. This 'stairway' allows us to exercise a degree of control over our emotions and think before we act. We are strengthening this connection every time we help

our child to calm down or reflect on their behaviour
and problem-solve.

Growing up is fundamentally about learning how to ensure
all these parts of the brain work together in harmony. Even
for adults, maintaining this balance is not always an easy
task – as any parent who has ever regretted firing off
an angry email to a teacher or shouting at their child
in the supermarket knows. For young children, managing
emotions is made many times harder by the fact that their
'upstairs' brains are not yet fully developed. They are
therefore much more vulnerable to being hijacked by big
feelings arising in the 'downstairs' brain at any time – what
Dr Siegel calls 'flipping your lid'.

The 'downstairs' brain is so powerful because it governs
the 'fight-or-flight' response that evolved to keep us alive –
and which can easily get triggered by the stresses of
everyday life, as we saw in Step 1. When the 'smoke alarm'
in our child's brain has been set off in this way, the 'stairway'
that normally allows the 'upstairs' brain to control strong
impulses is blocked. Messages can no longer pass between
the two levels – it's as if their brain has filled up with smoke.

Full-blown tantrum or calculated strategy?

As any parent knows, there are different types of meltdowns.
At times, a child may deliberately turn on the tears and

screams as part of a calculated strategy to try to get what they want. This is the 'upstairs' brain – which thinks and plans – in action. It's usually easy to tell such a performance from the real thing, but if you're in any doubt, take five deep breaths and ask your 'inner parent' for guidance. At other times, a child won't be able to control themselves because their 'downstairs' brain has taken over. If their fight-or-flight response has been triggered in this way, then your child won't be able to listen to your attempts to reason with them because the 'upstairs' brain that processes language and logic has gone offline.

Children who have 'flipped their lid' like this often tell me that they felt so overwhelmed and confused that they didn't know what they were doing. They had become so upset that they weren't able to grasp how much their behaviour had affected their parents. Some mums and dads find this surprising: how could they not remember the horrible things they said? Or the toy they threw at their sibling? But children may genuinely not know the answers to these questions. When they've been hijacked by their 'downstairs' brain, the logical prefrontal cortex has gone offline. They can no longer think through the consequences of their actions.

This loss of control can be accompanied by deep feelings of shame. Children realize they have let their parents down and can sense their disappointment. After they calm down, they may say the following sorts of things:

- 'I don't know why I hit him.'

- 'I don't remember lashing out.'

- 'I blacked out.'

- 'I can't control my temper.'

- 'I feel very sorry for what I did.'

- 'I feel ashamed of myself.'

- 'I feel bad for being naughty.'

Teaching your child about their brain

Whether or not they suffer from major meltdowns or anxiety, it can be enormously empowering for all children to learn about their brains. Strong feelings of sadness, anger and fear can be very frightening for young kids. Teaching them how their brain works helps them to handle their emotions more skilfully and make better choices in stressful situations, whether it's having a tantrum at bedtime, an argument with a friend or pre-exam nerves. Children love it when they start to realize that they don't need to live in fear of their big feelings: managing them is a skill they can develop. Learning about the brain can help transform feelings of blame and shame into a greater sense of confidence and control for you and your children.

Explain to your child that their feelings of anger or anxiety are their brain's way of trying to keep them safe. Our brains developed over millions of years to protect us from danger by sending signals to the body to make us faster, stronger and more powerful whenever they sensed any kind of threat. That's why we feel changes in our body like our heart beating faster, our breathing getting quicker, or butterflies in our tummy when we are stressed.

The problem is that the amygdala – our brain's 'smoke alarm' – is so sensitive that it often puts our body on red alert in situations where our lives are definitely not in danger. That's why manageable problems can seem so overwhelming. Our brains are treating our worries about school or an annoying sibling as if our lives are at risk, when in reality we are perfectly safe. When the panicky 'downstairs brain' has taken over, our anger and fear can feel so strong that we can't hear what our much more sensible 'upstairs brain' is trying to tell us. Normalize your child's feelings by explaining that everyone gets overwhelmed at times. It's nobody's fault if their brain sets off a false alarm.

Keep it simple and fun. I find children like to give the 'upstairs' brain, the 'downstairs' brain and amygdala ('smoke alarm') the names of characters to make them seem more 'real'. This is the approach used by MindUP™, a neuroscience-based programme to promote better learning developed by the Hawn Foundation in the United States, and also available in the United Kingdom.

In the MindUP™ curriculum, the amygdala is known as the brain's 'security guard' protecting us from danger. The 'upstairs' brain (or prefrontal cortex) is the 'wise leader' that helps us to make good decisions through reflection and problem solving. Children learn that when the 'security guard' goes into action it can be harder for the 'wise leader' to stay in control. We make mistakes when the 'wise leader' is no longer in charge.

These are the times when we need to take a five-minute 'brain break', take five deep breaths, or listen to soothing music until the 'wise leader' can get back in charge. Encourage your children to come up with their own names for these different parts of the brain and figure out the kinds of activities that help them to stay in control.

What to do when your child flips their lid

No matter what we do, there will be times when our child loses it. It's much easier to handle these situations if you have already had a think about how to respond when your child 'flips their lid'.

The first thing to do when confronted with your child's meltdown is to check in with yourself. Notice the sensations in your body and the kinds of thoughts popping into your head. Take five deep breaths. Your ability to remain as centred as you can is the single greatest antidote to your child's distress. Once you feel calmer, it will be easier to consult your 'inner parent' and consciously choose what to do to help your child cope.

Of course, this is not always easy. One of the problems with tantrums is that they can so easily prove contagious. If we're not careful, we can find that our child's meltdown triggers our own 'smoke alarm' – especially if we're already having a bad day or feel that everything's going wrong. Before we know it, we're stuck in a shouting match with our screaming, tearful child. Afterwards, we may feel racked with guilt and question our own judgement, wondering why it was so hard for us to keep our cool.

How to help your child calm down

If your child is in the grip of a 'downstairs' brain meltdown, then it's no use trying to use logic and reason to explain to them that what they're doing is wrong. You can't talk them out of feeling this bad. When the 'stairway' between the 'upstairs' and 'downstairs' brain has filled up with smoke, they won't be able to understand what you're saying.

There is no ready-made formula for helping any one child to calm down. What works will depend on the situation and your individual child. When you find yourself facing your child's meltdown, take a moment to pause and silently ask yourself:

- What do I need in this moment?

- What does my child need?

If you can be still for a few seconds, you will find your 'inner parent' knows what to do.

Power of a hug

Holding your child close to you can be comforting as long as you are feeling calm and in control yourself. Even though a part of you may resist the idea of rewarding your child for their unacceptable behaviour, you will be better placed to soothe them if you can put your own hurt and frustration aside. You can deal with the fact that you didn't like the way they behaved later. Giving them a hug or holding them close to you also releases oxytocin, the bonding hormone, which promotes a feeling of well-being and reduces production of the stress hormone cortisol. As we saw in Step 1, a hug also stimulates the Vagus nerve, which helps bring their stress levels back into balance.

Of course, this 'tend-and-befriend' approach – to use the term coined by Dr Shelley Taylor – does not work for all children at all times: some won't like to be touched when they are in the midst of a meltdown, particularly older children, though they might appreciate a hug afterwards. Your 'inner parent' will know when a hug is the best response.

Below are some more possibilities for responding to tantrums that other parents have found helpful.

Before the tantrum strikes

- **Know your child's triggers.** Identify the times or situations that make a tantrum most likely and try to minimize the build-up of stress where possible.

Perhaps your child is more vulnerable after a long day at school, after playing on their Xbox, or when they're hungry, tired or excited. When you know from past experience what kinds of situations are likely to cause problems, you can be on the lookout for signs that things are escalating and try your best to calm your child down before they hit the point of no return.

- **Reflect feelings.** Show you are trying to understand with statements like, 'I can see you are getting frustrated and annoyed right now,' or 'I know it's hard when I interrupt your computer game to ask you to come to the table.' Empathizing at this early stage helps a child feel heard and can defuse a build-up of resentment before it gets out of hand.

- **Burn off excess energy.** Children need plenty of opportunities to use up all their masses of energy – but most kids are sat at classroom desks all day. Children will be calmer after a good run around or a few minutes of dancing, rough-and-tumble play or sports. Maybe they need to roll around on some cushions or beanbags, have a go on a trampoline or to play outside in the fresh air for a few minutes. There is a growing body of research reinforcing what our parents' generation is fond of telling us: children tend to be more well-balanced and healthier if they are given regular opportunities to immerse themselves in nature. Even if you live in a built-up area, making time to explore a park or tear across a green can make a big difference.

● **Teach your child about their brain.** Children love to learn about their brains. Tell them about their 'upstairs brain' and their 'downstairs brain' and how to recognize the strong emotions that mean their amygdala – the brain's 'smoke' alarm – has been triggered. Treat each of these parts of the brain like different characters with their own names to make it more fun.

In the heat of the moment

● **See through your child's eyes.** Remind yourself that your child's distress is genuine, even if their problem appears insignificant. Although they may seem to be over-reacting to a trivial issue, their frustration is very real.

● **Speak softly.** When your child is having a tantrum, your ability to provide a calm presence is more powerful than anything you can say. It can work well to speak in low, soothing and comforting tones.

● **Get down to their level.** For younger children, it might be helpful to sit or crouch down next to them, speaking gently.

- **Distraction.** Distracting a child can be very effective as it activates the seeking part of the 'downstairs' brain. Engaging their curiosity in this way can release dopamine, a feel-good chemical that reduces stress and helps them feel interested and motivated.

- **Breathe the anger.** Imagine with your child that a fire has gone off in their brain and you are going to help them blow all those flames away.

- **Get them moving.** As Dr Siegel points out, getting a child moving has a direct effect on their brain chemistry, helping them to calm their fight-or-flight response and regain the ability to focus. Give your child space to move or breathe deeply before you attempt to talk about what just happened.

- **Take a break.** With an older child, you could say something like, 'We are both starting to get angry here. Shall we both take time out to calm down, then talk about this later when we can come up with a better solution?' State clearly that this is for a set time – say fifteen minutes – to ensure your child knows you are not abandoning them or running away from the problem. Returning to resolve the dispute after the break shows your child that you can work things out together, and models the kind of conflict-resolution skills that will serve them well as adults.

In the aftermath

- **Post-tantrum analysis.** When your child has calmed down, take the opportunity to engage their 'upstairs' brain to think through what has just happened, what they could have done differently and what they have learned. You can also take a moment to ask yourself if you might approach a similar situation differently in the future.

- **Really Listen.** When you run through what happened with your child, listen to their side of the story and resist the temptation to interrupt and argue if you do not agree. Allow them to share their perspective. (See pages 69–75 for tips on better listening.)

- **Validate.** Give your child permission to feel angry and explain that anger is a normal, healthy emotion. For example, 'I would feel angry too, if that had happened to me. I can understand why you got angry – it sounded like it felt really unfair for you, but screaming and hitting your sister is not the right way to deal with it.' Children need to learn that lashing out, swearing or hitting people is not okay – and that anger can be channelled in more positive ways, such as by burning off energy through exercise or play.

● **Learn and grow.** Take each meltdown as an opportunity to help strengthen connections in your child's 'upstairs' brain, rather than slipping into cycles of blame and shame.

● **Forgiveness.** Perhaps the best thing you can do for yourself and your child is to forgive yourself when you inevitably do lose your temper or find it difficult to remain calm. These are not easy situations to manage – and it's important to give yourself credit for doing the best you can.

Carly: 'He doesn't seem to hear me'

'When Leo's in a meltdown I keep asking, "What's wrong? What's the matter?" But he doesn't seem to hear me. I get extremely frustrated and often think it's my fault. I feel a real sense of failure for not being able to keep my child under control. Then I end up losing my temper with him and before I know it we're both screaming at each other. I hate to admit it, but at times like this I feel a real hostility towards my own child. When he's calmed down, I ask him again what was the matter and he says he doesn't know. I feel like I'm pressurizing him because he genuinely can't come up with an answer. I can tell he feels like he's let me down, and that makes me feel even worse.'

Continued . . .

When Carly gains a greater understanding of the way Leo's 'upstairs' brain has gone blank during his meltdown, she sees that reasoning with him won't work. Even more importantly, she sees that it's vital to manage her own reaction – so she doesn't go into fight-or-flight mode as well. Carly realizes Leo's outbursts are not a sign of failure on either side: if anything they are proof that the fight-or-flight mechanism that has kept our species alive is in full working order. We can't teach a child much when their 'downstairs' brain has taken over. But by working through what happened afterwards, Carly can help Leo develop the crucial 'upstairs' brain skills that will help him gradually to learn how to manage his emotions more successfully.

The next time Leo begins to lose it, Carly takes five deep breaths and watches her own response to his screams and sobs: a feeling that she's tensing up all over and getting hot. By remaining aware in this way, she has a better chance of staying calm even as Leo is consumed by anger. Carly notices that when she doesn't allow her own reaction to spiral out of control, Leo's behaviour doesn't seem quite as distressing. She's no longer gripped by feelings of failure – and sometimes Leo seems to calm down quicker than he did in the past.

'I'm definitely not perfect – I still sometimes lose my temper when Leo's screaming. I can still get in a real mood with him. But I've hung a picture of a heart up on the kitchen wall: it's a symbol of how much I love Leo despite everything. Whenever I start to feel myself getting angry, seeing the heart reminds me to take a moment to step back and remember that it's not going to help me or Leo if I'm unable to show him how to stay calm.'

Further possibilities

Here are some strategies that other parents have used to help their children gradually learn to better manage their feelings over time:

- **Meltdown diary.** Make a note of when tantrums occur to see if there are any patterns that reveal triggers which can then be avoided. The key questions are:

  - What caused the tantrum?
  - Can you identify specific factors such as being hungry, tired or hot, or feeling overwhelmed by something that happened at school?
  - What kind of behaviour did your child display?
  - What were the consequences of the behaviour?

One mum realized that her child's rages tended to erupt when *she* was feeling most stressed – particularly at the end of a workday. Seeing clearly that the meltdowns were linked to her own moods helped this mum give herself permission to take more frequent breaks. By showing herself greater kindness in this way, she was able to remain calmer – benefiting both herself and her son.

- **Anger thermometer.** Get some pens, paper and coloured card and work with your child to make a picture of an 'anger thermometer' with a gauge going from 0 (calm) to 10 (when their anger has exploded like a volcano). You can use this as a tool to connect with your child by exploring how their anger works. Begin by discussing what triggers your child's anger. Typical triggers might include:

    - Tiredness
    - Hunger
    - Being told to do something that they don't want to do
    - A particular time of day
    - A hard day at school/exam stress
    - Difficulties with friendships or a particular teacher
    - Stress over homework
    - Spending too long playing on screens
    - Fighting with siblings

Then discuss how their anger builds up by talking through specific examples of when they lost their temper. Ask them to identify the warning signs in terms of physical sensations in their body and assign a number from the anger thermometer to reflect the intensity of the feeling that goes with it. These are some of the common signs children have described to me, but there are many others:

- Foot starts tapping
- Fidgeting
- Feeling hot
- Breathing fast and shallow
- Muscles tense and jaw clenches

Next, ask your child about the kinds of thoughts that make them angry. Perhaps they feel they have been treated unfairly, a brother or sister is annoying them, or they don't want to be told what to do by adults.

It's helpful to ask them to chart their 'point of no return' – the number on the thermometer where they have become so angry that it is impossible for them to calm down and they need to be left alone for a few minutes before they can begin to settle.

Next time anger builds, encourage your child to describe the intensity of their feeling by saying a number from the thermometer. This will help them to catch themselves and interrupt the cycle.

This exercise is even more powerful if you work through your own anger thermometer in parallel. This helps to normalize anger and creates a space for you both to support each other to manage your moods. For example, if you're feeling under strain you can tell your child, 'I'm on a five now', and they will be able to understand clearly what's going on for you.

Talking through thoughts and feelings in this way helps your child to engage their 'upstairs' brain and start to become more self-aware. With your help, they can recognize their warning signs earlier and increasingly learn to manage their feelings. Rather than being a source of shame, each new meltdown is another opportunity to learn more about how their anger works.

● **Glitter jar.** The psychologist Dr Christopher Willard recommends a novel exercise: work with children to make a 'glitter jar' out of a plastic water bottle or jar. Choose three differently coloured glitters – one for thoughts, one for feelings and one for impulses to act on feelings (and maybe add some food colouring for fun). Shake the jar and show the children how confused the pattern becomes. Ask them to imagine what kind of events could cause the equivalent chaos in their minds. Being late for school? An argument with a sibling? Being told off by a teacher? Then show them what happens as they remain quiet and still: their thoughts, feelings and impulses gradually settle. The idea is to demonstrate the advantage of pausing before you act.

● **Visual cues.** In some schools, teachers agree to give certain children special cards that they can show the teacher when they are feeling overwhelmed and need a moment of quiet. Some parents use the cards at home with children to help them manage their anger. You could also agree that your child will use a special hand signal – such as a raised palm – if they're struggling to cope or sense a meltdown building.

● **A quiet den.** If you have enough space, create a special place with blankets, cushions or a favourite cuddly toy where a child can retreat if they need to calm down. This need not take up too much room: one mum allowed her young daughter to go and sit in a wardrobe, which they had agreed she would use when she needed a moment to cool down.

● **Label.** Working with younger children to label their feelings helps them to learn to handle their emotions better. This is best done when they have calmed down enough to engage their 'upstairs' brain. For example, if your child has just had a meltdown, you could ask them what words would best describe how they felt, such as 'angry', 'sad' or 'frustrated'. The act of naming feelings in this way helps children to learn to handle them when they occur in the future. You can also use visual cues to help your child describe what they were experiencing: pictures, books, 'feeling flashcards' or a 'feelings jar'. (For further reading, see Resources, page 261.)

● **Name or draw anger.** Younger children in particular may find it helpful to draw their anger or give it a name. Expressing their feelings by drawing brightly coloured scribbles, blobs and splotches can be a healthy, creative way to let off steam. Some children may also enjoy drawing their anger as a scary monster or a villain from a favourite story or film.

'Worry Monsters' and 'Bully Planets'

Drawing worries as figures such as a fairytale 'Worry Monster' or cartoon character can help children to put some distance between themselves and their concerns, and enable them to see worrying as a habit they have acquired, not an integral part of who they are.

For example, when I asked ten-year-old Ella to try to come up with a name for her stream of negative thoughts, she spontaneously said, 'Bully Planet' – visualizing a sinister-looking celestial object beaming self-critical thoughts into her mind. Though this might sound like a disturbing image, it was immensely liberating for Ella to start to think about her worries in this new way. Whenever Ella started to worry, she was able to tell herself, *'Bully Planet's taking over again,'* which immediately put some distance between herself and her worrisome thoughts. Or, when Ella was too upset to remember to say this, her mother asked her, *'Is Bully Planet saying nasty things again?'*

Eventually, Ella was able to enter into a dialogue with Bully Planet, saying, *'I'm not listening to you! Stop trying to make me feel bad! I don't believe everything you say!'* In one session, she wrote down what Bully Planet was saying then screwed up the paper and threw it into a rubbish bin. Of course, such an exercise is not a permanent 'cure' for worrying – but it helped Ella to feel that she was more in control of her negative thoughts and feelings.

Understanding the teenage brain

It used to be commonplace to blame teenagers' mood swings or irritability on their 'hormones'. But neuroscientists have learned more in recent years about how the adolescent brain undergoes a very distinct phase of development. As Adriana Galván, an associate professor at the University of California, puts it: from the point of view of brain science, teenagers are neither 'overgrown children' nor 'mini-adults'. Though neuroscience is still a very young discipline, it does seem that something quite unique is going on inside teenagers' skulls that influences the way they think, feel and behave.

In younger children the brain rapidly forms new neural pathways until the age of about twelve, when it starts removing connections it no longer needs, like a gardener snipping at a rosebush. This 'neural pruning' continues throughout the teenage years. The remaining connections are made faster through a process known as 'myelination', in which neurons are insulated with a sheath of fatty material. Because the brain develops from the back to the front, this upgrading process does not reach the prefrontal cortex – the 'upstairs' brain responsible for rational decision-making and self-control – until the twenties. Neuroscientists believe that evolving teenage brains are therefore incapable of exercising the same degree of judgement and self-control as adults – which won't be news to anybody with a teen living under their roof.

The way their brains develop seems to have a number of implications for the way teenagers behave:

- **Disregard for consequences.** Dr Daniel Siegel argues that teens are good at examining facts, but they can't always see the big picture of what might happen if they take a certain course of action. Though they may be fully aware of risks, they place more weight on the exciting potential benefits of taking a chance than what might happen if it all goes wrong. The limbic system in a teenage brain – which helps govern emotion – seems to derive more pleasure from risk-taking than an adult's does. With the logical prefrontal cortex still not fully developed, this may help explain why teenagers can be so impulsive.

• **Sensitivity to peer pressure.** According to the neuroscientist Professor Sarah-Jayne Blakemore, teenagers may be so acutely sensitive to their peers' opinions partly because their brains register the impact of being ostracized more acutely than adult brains. This helps explain why a teenage boy can easily succumb to pressure to smoke marijuana despite being fully aware of the risks, or why a teenage girl may give in to demands to send a naked selfie, even when she knows what could happen if the picture is shared. The desire to belong far outweighs fear of potential consequences.

• **Difficulty in seeing another's perspective.** The ability to 'mentalize' – or see a situation from another person's point of view – is still developing in teens. Neuroscientists have seen different patterns of brain activity in the teen brain compared to an adult brain during tasks that require thinking of others. One possible explanation is that teens use completely different strategies in social decision-making than adults. This might help explain why so many parents feel so exasperated with teenagers who seem incapable of seeing things from their point of view.

- **Interpretation of facial expressions.** Research by Dr Yolanda van Beek and Dr Judith Semon Dubas has provided intriguing evidence that teenagers may interpret facial expressions differently to adults. Their neuro-imaging experiment revealed that teens who were shown a picture of a neutral face experienced activation of their amygdala – the brain's 'smoke alarm' – creating a strongly negative reaction. In adults, the same photograph activated only the prefrontal cortex – the rational part of the 'upstairs' brain. Similarly, research by Dr Deborah Yurgelun-Todd suggested that teenagers have difficulty reading the faces of the adults around them. These findings could help explain why teens can be so hypersensitive and why they misinterpret neutral expressions from parents or teachers as signs of hostility.

Of course, it wouldn't make sense to reduce the accumulated research of the world's top neuroscientists into an excuse for reckless teenage behaviour. But it may make this behaviour easier to explain. An understanding of the teenage brain can also help us to have realistic expectations of our children. Remember: your child's brain will not be fully developed until they are twenty-five. The parts of the brain that support memory and forward planning are still very much a work in progress. So when they forget their gym kit for the tenth time in a row, despite your repeated reminders, don't take this as a sign of failure on your part, but a reminder that in many respects, it is up to parents to play the role of a teenager's 'upstairs' brain on their behalf. It takes patience and persistence, but you are the one with the life experience to coach them to think through consequences, get organized or resist peer pressure to take dangerous risks. These kinds of conversations will not only help keep your teen out of trouble, but will also boost their brain by reinforcing neural connections associated with discernment and self-control.

Teenage sleep: out of sync

In my work with teenagers, I've often been struck by the sheer numbers who seemed barely able to keep awake during our sessions. It was only relatively recently that I realized this wasn't a commentary on my failure to share their enthusiasm for the latest YouTube vlogger or bluff my way through Fortnite. When I asked them about their goals for our work together, they would often reply – yawning – 'To help me sleep.' Teenagers' traditional reluctance to drag themselves out of bed has tended to be treated as evidence of laziness. But researchers are starting to understand that there may be very real biological reasons why so many teens struggle to get up in the morning.

At about the age of ten to twelve, the release of melatonin – the hormone that aids sleep – shifts forward by roughly two hours, making it more difficult for teenagers to go to sleep and get up early. According to sleep researchers at the University of Oxford, asking a teen to get up at 7 a.m. to start school at 9 a.m. is a little like asking a fifty-five-year-old to get up at 5 a.m. No wonder, then, that so many teenagers feel sleepy well into mid-morning and seem to need such long lie-ins at weekends.

Though there's a strong biological case for teens starting lessons later, schools don't look likely to change their timetables any time soon. One way to reduce teenage sleep deficits might be to try to limit evening use of tablets or phones, which emit a low-level light in the blue wavelength that alerts the biological clock and may make it harder to sleep. Studies have also shown that using technology such as e-readers in the hour prior to sleep can delay the release of melatonin. Helping teenagers to learn about the importance of getting into a good sleep routine may help them to mitigate the worst effects of lost shut-eye.

The five key points

Teach your child about their brain

- Kids love to learn about their brains: it makes them feel more in control.

- Screaming and tears may be a sign the 'downstairs' brain has taken over.

- Anger and anxiety are contagious: check in with yourself when faced with your child's tantrum.

- Pause and ask, 'What do I need? What does my child need?'

- Teenage brains are different: try not to take their behaviour too personally.

Step
8

Be a safe haven from stress at school

Pick up almost any newspaper these days, and you will see a story about worrying levels of mental health problems in classrooms. More and more children and teenagers suffer from crippling anxiety attacks, low self-esteem, depression, chronic problems with concentration, eating disorders, worries over body image or self-harm. It's not just kids who are feeling the strain – it's their teachers too. In my work with families, I see so many children, teens and their parents who are struggling because of the pressures they are under at school.

Seeing their children suffer in this way can be especially painful for mums and dads who contrast their childhood memories of running around the park and climbing trees with today's packed schedules and ever-increasing homework. We worry about the impact of screens on developing brains, or whether our children will cope with the pressures of social media – new challenges that weren't around when we were growing up. Parents can feel particularly anxious to ensure that their children get to their first-choice school – and even if they do, they may wonder if it's the right environment for them. We're living in a society where the gap between haves and have-nots is very wide, and many parents feel immense pressure, and go to extraordinary lengths, to give their child every imaginable chance of success.

It's perhaps no coincidence that demand for professional support for children and teenagers facing emotional difficulties is increasing. Exam stress is one of the most common problems I see, driven by the growing pressure on students to perform from a young age and fears of what may happen if they don't get the right grades. Even very young children have started telling me about their tests, worried that their entire future rests on their next set of grades – a huge burden to carry at such a tender age. One teacher friend told me that she wasn't allowed to say 'great job' to pupils any more because the message always had to be: 'you could do better'. It's no coincidence that stress levels among teachers are soaring and their suicide risk is higher than in the general population. What kind of environment is this for our young people – with even their educators never feeling like they make the grade?

The tragedy is that a sense of feeling 'not good enough'

has become endemic among our kids. Those children whose talents may not necessarily easily translate into exam success end up believing they have let themselves down, regardless of the amount of effort they have put in. I will always remember one teenage girl I worked with who really struggled with maths. She was predicted to get an E at GCSE but managed a C because she worked so hard. This was a wonderful achievement but she still felt like a failure because she had not achieved an 'all-important' A. Even the most academically inclined kids can suffer the same lack of self-esteem, living in constant fear of missing the perfect grades they think they need to succeed in life, or of letting themselves, their parents, and their school down. Our society seems to have embraced such a narrow concept of 'success' – academic achievement, money and career – that so many kids with so much else to offer feel excluded before they have even had a chance to start making their unique contribution.

In my view, the alarming rates of mental health problems among young people are mirroring wider stresses in society and collective fears about the future. With so many uncertainties ahead, it's even more vital that our children and teens learn the importance of looking after themselves. I emphasize that their mental health and well-being is just as important as their exam results. The concept of 'self-care' is a new thing for many parents as well as kids, but it's something we all need to learn if we're going to meet the challenges to come.

The one great positive is that in my experience, today's children and teens can be incredibly self-aware. The young people that come to me are typically far more willing to talk about their problems than their parents. Opening up in this way takes enormous courage, but it's the first step towards confronting problems and building a life filled with greater wisdom, purpose and meaning. Parents can support this process by making sure their kids feel heard. We might not be able to change the school system overnight, but we can do all we can to make sure our homes are a safe haven from whatever pressures the outside world throws at our children.

Beth: 'I feel shocked and helpless'

When Beth's fifteen-year-old daughter Emily first came to see me, she walked into the room with downcast eyes and hunched shoulders, and hid her face behind her hair. She barely spoke, but when she did, she tugged the sleeve of her sweater over her hands. Beth's concerns reflected many of the issues I often see in my practice:

'I'm worried because Emily's coming up to her GCSE year. She's in the top sets for Maths and English, but she lacks confidence. She won't go out without make-up because she thinks everyone's staring at her – it's got so

Continued . . .

bad I'm actually seriously thinking about getting her to get her eyebrows and eyelashes dyed so we can actually get out of the house on time.

'And this is the bit that really shocks me. I've discovered she's been self-harming. I was stunned. I'd never heard of this before. How could anybody want to cut themselves with a razor? Let alone my daughter – she was such a sweet little girl at primary school. Whenever she disappears into her bedroom, I'm really worried that she might do it again. I feel I've maybe gone to an extreme, but I've locked everything sharp away. I don't know if that's really the right thing to do, if I'm making the right choices here. I just want her to go to school and build some confidence. It destroys me that she's hurting herself.

'My husband says that I've always been over-protective and that Emily's too dependent on me. He's probably right, but the minute I back off she has a melt-down and what mum stands back and lets her daughter fall apart? Even simple things end up being a problem. For example, I'd like her to go down to the shop and get me a few things, but she won't even go into our local Tesco's because she thinks everyone's looking at her. Even if I go with her she thinks she'll see girls from her school and they'll start post-ing nasty comments about her on Facebook.

'It's so different to when I was younger. I was bullied, but at least then you only had to deal with it during *school time. Now it continues out of hours, and it's into the weekend as well. I really feel for Emily, my heart goes out to her. I don't think I could have coped with that when I was younger.*

'I feel like a bad mum, and that I've somehow caused all this. It's all very well reading the advice, but the fact is that it's hard to stop beating yourself up and blaming yourself when things go wrong with your child. I bought a meditation CD, hoping that it would help to calm my nerves, but it just made me feel like more of a failure, because I couldn't empty my mind and stop thinking about my daughter. Emily's always texting me when I'm at work or I'm in meetings. How do you manage that? She needs to stop needing my reassurance so much. She's too dependent on me, she's just a mess, and to be honest I am too. All I want is for Emily to be happy.'

How to support your kids at exam time

It's normal to feel some anxiety ahead of exams, and a bit of stress can help us to keep focused and sharp. But too much worry can make our lives miserable and stop us performing at our best.

When looking for ways to support your child, try to address specific issues that are bothering them, normalize any nervousness they may be feeling and find out the best practical ways in which you can support them. Helping them find a suitable study space is obviously important, whether they enjoy silence or prefer to work with music or television in the background. Some young people may want to be left largely to their own devices, others may appreciate you showing solidarity by bringing them snacks and drinks when they are up late studying. Providing heartfelt praise for the effort they put in is important too. It's easy to forget that older children need to feel those expressions of delight over the determination they show that we may have more easily expressed when they were little ones.

Anxiety can quickly spread within a family, so it's important to try to keep your cool even if your child is feeling the strain. By providing a kind, nurturing presence, you can model the kind of self-care that will serve them well in later life.

Here are some practical tips:

- **Make space to listen.** The best thing you can do for your child is to make sure they know you'll be there for them if they want to talk – and that you're on their side. It's easy to assume we know what's going on in our child's head, but sometimes we might jump to the wrong conclusions. Take time to ask your child about any specific worries they have. Let them vent their frustration if they are struggling with revision or want to vent about an exam that didn't go as well as they had hoped. Sometimes the greatest gift you can give is the silence of your undivided attention – even if only for a few minutes. They don't expect you to have all the answers, but this kind of supportive listening can be more valuable than any words you say.

● **Remember their fear of disappointing you.** Of course, there may be times when you need to encourage a child to revise, and many parents know it can be an uphill struggle if they're having difficulty focusing. But too much pressure can backfire. Mums and dads I work with are often surprised when they find that their son or daughter is worried about whether they will let them down. Even young people who seem defiant or rebellious may be hiding a deep fear of not living up to their family's expectations. The most important message parents can convey is that the loving bond you share has nothing to do with grades. Making sure they know you will be proud of them no matter how they do in their exams won't make them lazy: it will help motivate them even more.

● **Remind them that there are many paths to success.** Exams are important, and parents naturally want their children to do well. But we all know examples of people who didn't do well at school, but have gone on to have successful and happy lives. Many young people feel so stressed because they think that their entire future depends on this one chance at getting their grades. If your child is paralysed by a fear of failure, it can help to talk through their worries to put them into perspective. If they don't get the grades they were hoping for, you can work with them to consider their options, including the possibility of re-sits or looking at different routes or qualifications. It might seem to your child that their exam results are the end of the world, but as adults we know there are many paths to success.

● **Teen brains are different.** Some teens can be overwhelmed by anxiety or even suffer panic attacks when exams loom. It can seem like they are over-reacting, but it's worth bearing in mind that teenage brains are not fully developed until they reach their mid-twenties, as we saw in Step 7. The stress of exams often triggers their fight-or-flight response: the primitive fear mechanism that kept our caveman ancestors alive. If a teen is having a severe panic attack, it's a sign that they've gone into survival mode and they may not be able to take on board any reassurance you offer. Anxiety is contagious so the key thing is to stay centred yourself: this will help them to relax. Once they've calmed down, you can take some time to talk things through. (See below for more guidance on managing anxiety and panic attacks.)

● **Help them think differently about their worries.**
When young people start to worry, it's very easy for
them to get caught up in the negative chatter in their
head. Soon they are trapped in a spiral of self-critical
thoughts – none of which are necessarily helpful or
true. Common examples include:

> 'I'm never going to get this.'
> 'I'm useless.'
> 'I'm going to fail.'
> 'Everyone else is better than me.'
> 'I'll never forgive myself if I don't get A*s.'
> 'I shouldn't be this stressed.'

You can talk with your child to help them identify
these kinds of repetitive thoughts and encourage them
to find more helpful ways of thinking. Examples
include:

> 'I'm doing my best – and that's all I can do
> right now.'
> 'It's not nice to feel stressed, but it's normal to be
> nervous at exam time.'
> 'This won't last for ever and I've got things to look
> forward to in the summer.'
> 'I'll do as much revision as I can in the time I've got.'
> 'Things might come up in the exam that I don't
> know so well. I can still do my best.'

- **Give your child some space.** It can be difficult as a parent to strike a balance between helping your child to develop a healthy level of self-discipline and pushing them too hard. Micro-managing or nagging is never that helpful and it's important to know when to back off during exam season – even though this can feel like a hard thing to do. It's normal for your child to be snappy and moody. Tears and slammed doors may become part of daily life. Try to remember that your child is under immense pressure right now, and that the best thing you can do for them is to make sure they know you are there for them.

- **Manage your own expectations.** With so much pressure on children to do well, parents can start to feel stressed themselves. Try to notice whenever you are getting caught up in your own worries about your child's performance. Remember they are doing the best they can. By showing you trust and love them, regardless of how they do, you will be giving them firmer foundations than any grades can provide.

- **Beating procrastination.** Intense anxiety can cause us to avoid the situations we're worried about. For young people this can mean difficulties getting started with their revision – a sure sign they may be more anxious about their exams than they are letting on. With so much of a young person's social life taking place online via Facebook, Snapchat and other apps, it's easy for them to get distracted by computers or phones. Encourage them to put their devices away and suggest that they try just ten minutes of work to get started. Once they do finally get going, they may find it's easier than they feared.

● **Remind them to take a break.** Some young people may stay holed up in their bedroom cramming deep into the night. Explain that it's important to take regular short breaks, which will help their mind consolidate what they have just learned. Even a brisk walk up and down the street can work wonders for concentration. Some families find it helpful to sit down and agree a schedule: for example, everyone stops working at 8 p.m. to eat dinner together.

● **Offer practical support.** Start a conversation with your child about the kinds of practical things you can do to help, particularly in terms of giving them time and space to study. Try to avoid scheduling any big family events during exam season, and it never hurts to keep up regular deliveries of their favourite drinks and snacks. You may also be more lenient about their chores. Healthy, nutritious food is obviously important, especially a hearty breakfast on exam days.

● **Schedule rewards.** It can help to decide on some treats to help them get through their revision and give them something to look forward to once they've finished their exams. This could include things like tickets to see their favourite band or a summer music festival. They can also schedule 'mini-rewards' such as five minutes of watching YouTube videos for doing an hour of revision.

● **Help them get enough sleep.** Young people who are worried about their exams may have difficulty sleeping or stay up late to cram. Help them to get into a good sleep routine: you may need to make sure they put any phones or tablets aside an hour before bed, since they emit light in a frequency that may make it harder to fall asleep.

● **Show them the power of five deep breaths.** One of the simplest things you can do to help a child who is feeling overwhelmed is to remind them to breathe. By breathing in to a count of five, and breathing out to a count of five, we immediately help ourselves feel a little calmer. Young people can use this technique whenever they feel anxious, particularly before they start revision, when they're waiting outside the exam hall or just before they turn over their exam paper.

Try It: Naming feelings

One way to help both you and your child manage your feelings is the simple practice of naming how you feel. Research by the neuroscientist Dr Matthew Lieberman suggests that labelling emotions activates the prefrontal cortex – the rational part of the 'upstairs' brain – and calms the 'smoke alarm' in the amygdala. Dr Daniel Siegel calls this technique 'name it to tame it'. It's also the reason why chatting to a friend about difficult feelings, writing them down or talk therapy can be so helpful.

In dealing with a difficult child or teen, it is very easy to feel overwhelmed, disrespected, disappointed or upset. Such feelings are normal, but you don't have to let them control the way you respond. It can help to explain calmly to your child how you feel about their behaviour: *'I feel really disappointed/angry/hurt right now.'* By choosing to offer information about your feelings – rather than lashing out – you are providing your child with a model of how to handle difficult emotions with maturity.

Kim: 'I'll be happy if you do your best'

'My fifteen-year-old daughter, Amber, has no self-confidence and she's always talking about how she doesn't feel good enough. She doesn't like how she looks and now she's barely eating because she thinks she's fat – which she isn't. It breaks my heart that Amber feels like this. She's a perfectionist and she's determined to get into a good university. I don't put her under any pressure, but the teachers are pretty pushy at her school, and to be honest I think the other girls work each other up about their results. I tell her I'll be happy if she just does her best – but she doesn't see it like that. She feels that if she doesn't get it "right" now, she will have screwed up the rest of her life. There seems to be so much more pressure these days. It wasn't like that when I was young. We had no idea what we were going to do with the rest of our lives. I wouldn't have had a clue. I keep telling Amber that her well-being is the most important thing, but she says that's easy for me to say as I'm not the one taking my GCSEs. They were told at school that they aren't just competing with the others in the class – they are competing with every child in the country. It's a pressure I just couldn't believe.'

Anxiety and panic attacks

Anxiety is one of the most common problems I see among school-age children and teens, and studies suggest it's on the rise. Fortunately, there is a lot that can be done to help individuals suffering from anxiety, and it's worth checking out the many helpful organizations, online resources and books listed in the Resources section on pages 261–84.

Remember: anxiety can occur in a number of forms, from phobias to Obsessive Compulsive Disorder, so it's worth finding out which form a child or teen may be experiencing. Some young kids may get anxious when they are separated from their parents at the school gates, while others may feel unsettled by family difficulties or sudden losses such as a bereavement. In my work with families, I often encounter teenagers suffering from social anxiety, meaning they are paralysed by a fear of what others might think of them. While a degree of self-consciousness is normal in teens, some become so awkward and preoccupied with their fears of being judged as weird, stupid, boring, ugly or fat that it's not an exaggeration to say that they can barely function. They are desperate to fit in, but feel they don't belong. Although this kind of social anxiety is widespread, by far the most common cause of anxiety I see is the academic pressures children and teens are under at school.

Bear in mind that anxious kids may be reluctant to tell you that there is something wrong and they may even find it hard to understand or talk about what they are feeling.

As parents, we need to rely on our detective skills. Keep a careful eye out for physical symptoms: a child who is anxious about going to school may be more likely to complain of headaches or stomach aches than open up over exam fears or bullying. They may be experiencing shortness of breath, a racing heart or feeling shaky without knowing why. By finding time to sit down and talk to them you can help them to join the dots. Here are some other potential signs to watch for:

- Changes to sleep patterns
- Angry or tearful outbursts
- Shaky, sweaty or restless
- Worrying more than usual
- Problems concentrating
- Becoming withdrawn
- Loss of appetite
- Bed wetting
- Nausea or stomach cramps
- Loss of interest in activities they used to enjoy
- Seeking escape by excessively checking a phone

Helping your child to bring their anxiety under control

When our child is consumed with worry, we will naturally feel an urge to try to reassure them that they are blowing things out of proportion. It's vital to talk to your child, but many parents I work with say that their best attempts to offer comfort don't seem to work: their child can't seem to take anything they say on board.

As we saw in Step 7, when a child or teen is in the grip of intense feelings of anxiety or anger, their logical 'upstairs brain' may go offline, meaning they can't think about a problem logically. When their fight-or-flight response has been triggered in this way, the neurochemicals cascading through their system will be far more powerful than anything you can say. If your child's 'downstairs brain' has taken over, then constant reassurance can actually feed their fears, and keep the cycle of anxiety spinning. We need to support our child to put their 'upstairs brain' in control as much as possible. Here are some simple ways to help:

- **Five deep breaths.** Help your child to slow down their breathing. Encourage them to take five long, slow deep breaths to soothe the physical symptoms of anxiety in their body.

- **Teach them about the brain.** Explain that feeling anxious is just the brain's way of trying to keep them safe. Our brains evolved to protect us over millions of years, but sometimes they set off a 'false alarm' – causing us to worry far more than is helpful. For more on tackling anxiety by talking to your child about their brain, see pages 132–4 in Step 7.

● **Normalize their worries.** Children want to know that they are not going crazy, and that there is nothing wrong with them. Explain that worry is something we all experience from time to time.

● **Emphasize the value of having a go.** Anxious children will often avoid certain situations or activities because they are worried about making a mistake or not performing 'perfectly'. Make sure your child knows the value of trying new things and having fun, no matter whether they 'succeed' or 'fail'.

● **Worst-case scenarios.** Children with anxiety often focus on 'what ifs' or imagine worst-case scenarios. When your child is calm enough to think clearly, help them to change these patterns of thought by reminding them of all the times in the past when they felt anxious but things worked out okay in the end. Help them to challenge their irrational fears with facts and evidence. Build confidence by helping them plan how they will respond if things don't go the way they want.

● **Help them to problem-solve for themselves.** If we offer too much advice our children will become overly dependent and won't learn to problem-solve. Help them to come up with their own solutions by asking questions such as:

'What do you think might work?'
'What do you think might help this to be better?'
'What do you think would help?'
'What do you think the options are?'
'Would this option or that option be better?'

Young people may struggle to come up with answers at first, but if you help them to think through their options they will gradually learn to develop the kind of resourcefulness that will serve them throughout their lives.

● **Positive self-talk.** Just as we learned in Step 2 to challenge the 'frenemy' in our head, you can help your child to learn to observe the way their mind generates anxiety-creating thoughts. Work with them to think up some more positive phrases that they can write down and return to when they are feeling anxious. Here are some examples:

For facing a challenging situation:
'It's not going to be as bad as I think.'
'It won't be for long and I can cope with it.'
'I might even enjoy it if I go.'
'Let's just give it a try.'

For coping with a challenging situation:
'Just concentrate on what's happening.'
'Let's just relax and think positive.'
'This is just anxiety. It isn't nice but it can't hurt me.'
'I have done it before and I can do it again.'
'I am okay. I am safe. I can cope with this.'

Self-praise after the event:
'I did it, I coped!'
'I achieved that, I'm getting better.'
'That was tough, but I got through it.'
'It will be easier next time.'

● **Climbing the 'fear ladder'.** When working with anxious kids, I often use an approach called 'graded exposure' where I help them to slowly face their fear of a specific situation one step at a time, in a gradual and manageable way. We do this by making a 'fear ladder' – a diagram that shows how they can start with easier tasks to build up to scarier challenges.

We first identify what is making a child anxious. It may be as broad as 'going to school'. We then break the challenging situation into ten manageable chunks – each representing a specific step the child can take to climb the 'ladder'. For example, the lowest rung on the 'ladder' of 'going to school' may be 'going into a classroom with a teaching assistant while Mum waits for me at the school reception'. The second rung might be 'going into a classroom with a teaching assistant while Mum waits for me in the car outside', and so on. The highest rung may be 'going to school without any extra help'.

You can help your child to rate their anxiety on a scale of one to ten as they attempt each step (with zero meaning 'no anxiety' and ten meaning 'high anxiety'). As they master each rung they can gradually move through the most anxiety-provoking tasks on the ladder. Give them plenty of praise and encouragement at every step to help motivate them to keep going.

Panic attacks

For anybody who has never experienced a severe form of anxiety, it can be hard to grasp just how debilitating the condition can be. What starts as a background feeling of dread can rapidly spiral into a crippling fear that can leave a child or teenager afraid to take on simple tasks such as speaking in class, hanging out with friends or attending a family gathering. In some cases, anxiety can erupt into a full-blown panic attack – accompanied by sweating, a racing heart, hyperventilation and palpitations. The attack may last only a few minutes, but the fear can be so intense that sufferers can be convinced they are about to die.

If your child or teen suffers from panic attacks, here are a few points to bear in mind about what's going on – and how to respond:

- **Over-reaction.** Panic attacks happen when the body's fight-or-flight response has been triggered. The amygdala – the brain's 'smoke alarm' – is reacting as if you are in mortal danger, even though you aren't. This can create an overwhelming feeling of fear which can come on suddenly and last for about ten or fifteen minutes (although it may seem like much longer).

- **Catastrophic thinking.** The mind is misinterpreting the physical sensations that accompany anxiety as a sign of impending catastrophe. Young people suffering a panic attack may fear they are going to faint or suffer a heart attack.

- **Empathize.** Even if you've never had a panic attack yourself, don't underestimate how distressing they can be for your teen. Their brain is convinced they are facing mortal danger, even if they are completely safe.

- **Identify triggers.** Panic attacks are usually triggered by a certain situation, such as having to speak in front of class or taking exams. Discuss with your child or teenager whether they occur at specific times of day, such as late at night, when they are tired and feeling stressed about school the next day.

- **Soothe them.** During an attack, speak as calmly as possible and remain as centred as you can, perhaps by taking five deep breaths. Remind them that anxiety is a normal response (designed to prepare the body for danger) and that they have come through this before. Consider placing a calm picture – something they have chosen – in their room or on their phone. Remind them to take five deep breaths too.

- **Agree on a response.** Figure out with your child or teenager what would be most helpful for them if they are gripped by a panic attack and agree on a course of action in advance. Would they like you to remain with them, offering comforting comments or a rub on the back? Or would they prefer to be left alone? Perhaps going for a walk or exercising can help release the build-up of excess energy. It's important to agree on how you can respond to these attacks as a team.

As always, the key thing when confronted with a child or teenager in distress is to remain as calm as possible and provide the safe haven they need to feel secure.

Self-harm

Most common among teenage girls, self-harm usually involves some form of cutting arms or legs, usually with razor blades, though sometimes with knives, scissors or pins – or burning with cigarette lighters. There are usually strong feelings of secrecy, guilt and shame attached, and teens often fear telling parents because they feel they've let them down and that they won't understand.

Teenagers may feel very reluctant to confide in you, but they need to know that if they do try to talk to you they won't be judged, and that you can cope with what you're hearing. This isn't always easy: it's natural that self-harm can bring up a strong mix of feelings, and it can be hard to comprehend how or why a young person could do this to themselves. In their distress, many parents naturally fear that their child's self-harming is evidence that they want to take their own life. Although self-harm *can* be a risk factor for suicide, in the vast majority of cases I've seen the young person has no intention of killing themselves. They are usually trying to cope with intense emotions, and may even have been exposed to social media sites that romanticize self-harm. The behaviour becomes easier to understand when you consider that the brain circuits involved in physical pain are very closely related to those that govern emotional pain, so cutting can provide a temporary feeling of relief. These young people need help to find better ways to manage their feelings and become more emotionally resilient.

The best thing you can do when faced with such a situation is to nurture yourself as far as possible and be the non-judgemental, safe parent that your teen can open up to. Talking about it will not make it worse; it will provide a space where your teen can begin to explore their feelings.

Here are some additional pointers some parents find helpful:

- **Keep talking.** Since self-harm is often cloaked in strong feelings of shame, it's important to strike a balance between keeping a dialogue going and ensuring you don't put your child under too much pressure, which could make them even more secretive.

- **Identify triggers.** Talk with your child to find out what kinds of stressors make them more likely to self-harm – for example: arguments with friends, feelings of rejection, stresses over schoolwork, or bullying on social media.

- **Healthier outlets.** Help your child to find other ways to manage their unwanted feelings, such as exercise, writing, breathing, trampolining or playing an instrument. Encourage them to experiment with substitutes for self-harm, such as squeezing stress balls, pinging an elastic band on a wrist, drawing on an arm in red pen, screaming into a pillow or throwing socks against a wall. See if they can distract themselves from their urge to self-harm by setting a timer for ten minutes, using music or YouTube, or phoning a friend.

- **Seek support.** There are many groups, online resources and books for parents facing self-harm, and it may be that you and your child need professional support. (See Resources, page 261.)

Depression

Characterized by a persistent low mood, sadness and a general sense of apathy, depression is usually accompanied by a loss of interest in activities a teen usually enjoys. Sufferers may become withdrawn and spend a lot of time alone in their room. You may notice that they are self-critical, tearful, tired and often yawning a lot because they are having difficulty sleeping. They may also be irritable and suffer angry outbursts, and either lose their appetite or binge-eat. They may feel hopeless or suicidal and say things like, 'I wish it would all end.'

Sometimes it can be very difficult to tell the difference between a teenager who is going through a period of withdrawal or moodiness and somebody who is suffering from depression. Some teenagers become adept at hiding their chronic unhappiness because they fear being stigmatized or further alienated, or they may not want to be a burden on their families and friends. They may also be reluctant to seek help because they fear they are beyond hope and feel very alone. This is understandably very worrying for parents, particularly when you feel you can't get through to them. It's vitally important that a teenager suffering in this way finds somebody they can open up to. It may be that you will need to help them access professional help by consulting your GP. (For an excellent online resource on depression, see YoungMinds on pages 267–8.)

Sex and relationships

Young people will at some point start experimenting with their sexuality and dating. Although this is natural and inevitable, it can still be difficult as a parent to acknowledge that your teen is growing up. As with other issues confronting your teen, the key is to start a conversation about what makes a healthy relationship as soon as you feel they're ready. It goes without saying that some teens may find having these kinds of discussions with their parents excruciatingly embarrassing, but it's important to try to connect: you can provide vital information on the risks and responsibilities that sexual activity brings, and offer a mature perspective on what it means to respect yourself and others in relationships.

This is an emotive topic and it can bring up powerful feelings, especially if you feel your teen is putting themselves at risk or disrespecting you. As a parent, it's obviously important to set appropriate limits to keep your teen safe. If these boundaries are breached, try not to over-react, as this will only push your teen away and shut communication down. The more you can step back from your reactions, the greater your ability to ensure your teen feels heard, no matter how shocked you may feel. You can't control the decisions your teen will make about sex, but you can choose how to respond. If you can approach the situation calmly, you'll have a much better chance of working together to help your teen develop the maturity they will need to make good decisions – now and in the future.

Friendships

While the dramas of classroom friendships may seem trifling compared to adult concerns, the emotional stakes can be very real for children. It can be heart-rending as a parent to see your lovely daughter suddenly being ostracized for no apparent reason, or obsessed by the belief that her friends are much prettier or more popular, or to see your gentle son being mercilessly bullied – face-to-face or online. Young people can be very cruel, blanking each other or dishing out verbal abuse that can be as painful as physical blows.

The challenge is to know when to get involved and when to hold back. Friendships offer vital opportunities for children to learn to resolve conflicts, assert themselves and learn social skills that will be vital in adult life. Intervening too much can deprive them of these lessons. The most helpful thing is to provide a listening ear and gently help your child see that often their friends' behaviour says a lot more about them. You can ask whether somebody who is happy would behave in such a nasty way, and help a young person to see that whilst the 'popular ones' may appear to have many friends, it doesn't mean they are the most likeable people. Explain that bullies resort to their horrible behaviour to give them a feeling of being in control, often because they are hiding deep feelings of fear, anger or shame.

I have found that with a little encouragement some children and teens can come up with imaginative inner resources that help bolster their confidence. For example, I have worked with young people of different ages who use a variety of visualizations to feel 'protected' at school:

- **Shields, armour and force fields.** A mask that shoots out a force field of protection. An invisible bubble. Ivy vines that erupt and absorb unkind words. Medieval-style armour or shields.

- **Imaginary headphones.** To block out harsh comments. The wearer repeats the mantra: 'That's just their opinion – it doesn't make it true.'

- **Angel wings.** To bat away negative comments.

It can also be helpful to talk to a young person about being assertive rather than accepting bullying passively or lashing out in response. (See Resources, page 261.)

Body image

Across Britain, teenage girls are silently battling feelings of inferiority because they do not feel they measure up to the air-brushed versions of the feminine ideal promoted by the media and the fashion industry, or the carefully filtered selfies posted by their peers. I see this problem all the time: so many girls are convinced they are too fat, too thin, too short, too tall, or they don't like their nose, thighs, freckles or hair. Some suffer from serious eating disorders, such as bulimia or anorexia, and need specialist care. (A detailed exploration of these illnesses is beyond the scope of this book – there are some suggestions for further resources on page 274.) Many others simply live with the constant nagging voice of their 'inner critic', or even the cruel voice of bullies, telling them they are weird, ugly or fat. Increasingly, teenage boys are also falling prey to similar insecurities about whether their physique conforms to the ideals they see online or on TV. The distress of young people suffering in this way is a national shame, and heartbreaking for any parent.

It's easy to feel helpless in the face of such deep, collective pain, but I've been privileged to work with teens who have learned to appreciate that their inner qualities are far more important than how they look. This isn't necessarily an easy journey to make. Many teenagers can see right through our appearance-obsessed culture, but struggle to believe they will amount to anything or achieve any worthwhile goals in a society where looks count for so much. They know deep down that they will never look like a Victoria's Secret model or a Premier League footballer – and no amount of reassurance will convince them that they're good enough. As one teenage girl said to me, 'It's all very well saying I'm a kind, fun person to be around – but boys my age want someone who looks like Selena Gomez.' Indeed, it might not help to try to cheer up a teenage girl who's convinced she is ugly by saying, 'No you're not, you're so pretty.' Such a comment may be well intentioned, but it reinforces the idea that being 'pretty' is what matters most.

I try to help teens dig deeper and discover they are more powerful than they realize. By identifying their strengths and starting to pursue their dreams more fully, they can project an inner confidence that shines more brightly than any of the Photoshopped images they see in magazines. It can help to acknowledge the darker side of the fashion industry – and that many of the celebrities teenagers worship are going through their own struggles behind the glossy façade. Without needing to become harsh or aggressive, teenage girls can start to value their potential to grow into strong women who stand up for what they believe in, regardless of what anyone else might think. They can learn to appreciate their bodies less in terms of their looks and more in terms of health and vitality. Such changes will unfold more quickly when a parent can model the kind of self-acceptance they would wish for their child.

The problem for many parents is that they themselves have spent a lifetime battling an 'inner critic' who is similarly focused on their body-shape, and they may have struggled with their own relationship to food. As we saw in Step 2, the more we notice the 'inner critic' at work, the less influence it has over us. By learning to accept our own appearance, we can help our teenagers do the same. We can gradually create an environment that encourages them to adopt a more expansive view of themselves than the degree to which they might resemble Justin Bieber or Taylor Swift.

Here are some of the approaches I use when working

with teenagers and their families where body image is an issue:

- **Focus on inner strengths.** We refrain from complimenting appearance in favour of praising qualities such as kindness, how a teenager treats others or the effort they've put into something. Better to downplay the importance of looks altogether and focus on the inner strengths that allow a teen to contribute to the lives of their friends, family and community. We try to live by the same values, and become more aware of the potential message we may inadvertently send when we compare our own looks unfavourably with other people, or glance in the mirror and mutter, 'Ugh, I need to lose a few pounds.'

- **Praise vitality rather than appearance.** Rather than telling a teen how beautiful or good-looking they are, focus on their vitality or inner glow. I sometimes say to a teenager, 'Something is shining through you today.' It also helps if adults refrain from commenting too much on other people's appearance to avoid reinforcing the idea that looks are all-important.

- **Honest conversations.** Teens can seem so worldly in some respects that it's easy to forget that they may not fully appreciate realities that may be obvious to adults: the celebrities they admire are portrayed in carefully doctored images and accompanied by armies of personal trainers, beauticians, nutritionists and cosmetic surgeons – they are not living normal lives.

- **Discuss healthy eating and exercise.** It may be obvious to adults, but many teens don't grasp the importance of a balanced diet at this crucial time for the development of their body and brain. It can also help if the whole family adopts healthier routines in terms of exercise and diet, with a focus on feeling wholesome and energized rather than measuring weight.

- **Men have a role.** It's important for dads or other male relatives to play their part in supporting teenage girls and boys to appreciate their inner qualities and see through the illusions peddled by the advertising industry. Young men need role models who can show them that being a man is not about conforming to macho stereotypes or succumbing to peer pressure, but learning to trust their own judgement and respect themselves and others, particularly in the way they relate to women.

It's not easy to help teenagers stand apart from the corrosive aspects of our culture. Ultimately, the most important thing is to show them that the values they bring into the world in the way they live their lives are far more important than how they look.

Sensitive children

Over the years, I have come across many parents who say there is something 'different' about their child. Their son or daughter seems to be particularly sensitive and to feel things more deeply than other children. They can be acutely sensitive to sensory overload – especially loud noise or variations in temperature. They may burst into tears or throw tantrums easily, but also seem to think very deeply and have huge hearts. They might be particularly disturbed by news stories about global problems, suffering or injustice and seem burdened beyond their years. Though they may be highly intelligent, they may struggle to cope with the noise and bustle of a mainstream school and say they don't feel listened to or understood.

Teachers or mental health professionals often struggle to know how to categorize such children, who don't seem to fit an official diagnostic box such as autism or ADHD (see box, pages 194–6). I've worked with many parents who know their children are not suffering from some sort of disorder, but they do seem to require more understanding and nurturing than their peers, or even their siblings.

Dr Elaine Aron, an American psychologist, uses the phrase 'Highly Sensitive Person' (HSP) to describe such children, whom she estimates make up about 20 per cent of the US population. Though this is not a term commonly used in Britain, I have come across many such children, whom I have observed display a number of the following characteristics:

- Feels emotions more intensely than other children

- Highly sensitive to noise, taste, heat or other forms of sensory overload

- Takes things personally

- Very loving and wants to connect physically and emotionally

- Deep thinker who can get lost in their own world

- Has intense meltdowns

- Takes criticism to heart – and holds on to it for days

- Frequent worrying and anxiety

- Dislikes change

- Can burst into tears or lose their temper easily

- Highly empathic to other children's feelings

- Strong sense of fairness and justice

- Intense negative reactions to lying in any form

- Strong affinity with animals or passion for environmental issues

- Easily drained but may have difficulty sleeping

- Questions rules that don't make sense

- Highly attuned to what adults around them may be feeling

- Unusually sensitive to textures of clothing

Our society isn't geared to people with such sensitive temperaments, and these children don't tend to fit in easily to our existing schools. Because they tend to take things so personally, they can feel crushed by the kind of telling off or punishment that other children would take in their stride. As parents, we can see that such setbacks have a much greater impact on their self-esteem, and they may be especially prone to internalizing a negative view of themselves.

While we are naturally concerned about the emotional difficulties these sensitive children experience, we need to recognize the enormous potential their sensitivity, compassion and empathy hold for themselves, their families and the wider community. As a culture, we tend to see this kind of sensitivity as a weakness – even though these children's empathy for their fellow humans, animals and the environment might be precisely the qualities the world needs right now.

The American professors Thomas Boyce and Bruce Ellis argue that sensitive children can be viewed as 'orchids'. Like these beautiful, delicate flowers, these children are acutely sensitive to their environment. They can flower into unusually talented and creative adults if nurtured properly, but they can easily wither if they don't receive the right care. Most children, however, resemble 'dandelions' – they are far more resilient and can thrive in a wide range of environments. Boyce and Ellis are investigating whether genetic factors may play a role in whether a child is an 'orchid' or a 'dandelion', and how we can help all types of children to thrive.

There are no hard-and-fast rules for how to raise an 'orchid' child. What we can do, however, is to explore our own attitudes towards their sensitivity. Do we see it as a defect? Or can we embrace the unique contribution these children can make when they are accepted and understood? It's easy to get caught up in what seems to be 'wrong' with our child – but the more we can see them with fresh eyes and keep an open mind, the more we will come to appreciate the quirks and strengths that this degree of sensitivity brings. Even if others can't always see your child's gifts, trust your instincts. Your 'inner parent' knows the kind of nurturing and understanding your child needs. Though this is a new field, there are some great books on sensitive children and I have listed several on page 268 of the Resources section.

When a Child Is Diagnosed with ADHD

Growing numbers of children and teenagers are being diagnosed with Attention Deficit Hyperactivity Disorder (ADHD) or other neurodevelopmental disorders. Such a child will have significant difficulties in the following areas, in at least two environments (e.g. at home and at school), compared to another child of the same age and ability:

● **Hyperactivity.** Constantly fidgety, has difficulty sitting still, runs around a lot and is often restless at night.

● **Concentration.** Finds it very hard to focus on a task, follow instructions or complete things.

● **Impulsivity.** Acts without thinking through consequences, blurts things out, talks excessively and struggles to wait their turn.

(In some cases, where hyperactivity is not a problem, a child showing these symptoms may be diagnosed with Attention Deficit Disorder (ADD)).

Every child experiences their symptoms in different ways, but I find that parents whose child has ADHD tend to encounter a number of similar issues. Schools and individual teachers vary widely in the degree to which they understand these kinds of conditions, or even acknowledge that they exist. Some show the patience and care that can make all the difference, but others are less sympathetic – and may even assume ADHD is some sort of myth, or an excuse for bad behaviour. A child can end up being scapegoated and find themselves stuck with a label of the 'naughty one', the 'class clown' or the 'troublemaker'.

For parents, it's easy to slip into a sense of failure or to assume you're doing something wrong when your child proves difficult to manage. It can be hard to see their strengths when they are viewed as a 'problem' by their school, and painful when the system isn't geared up to provide the nurturing environment they need. In our fatigue and frustration, we can easily lose sight of the positives – and particularly the enormous energy and enthusiasm that children with ADHD can channel into their passions. It's no coincidence that there are many highly successful athletes, film stars, musicians and top executives in the business world who have this diagnosis.

As with any parenting challenge, the first task is to find your own calm centre before making any decisions. There are a lot of misunderstandings

Continued . . .

around ADHD and it's important to seek specialist advice and avoid any temptation to go online and diagnose your child yourself. Obtaining a professional diagnosis is essential to navigating the system and accessing the right help – a little like having a passport to visit a foreign country. But a label is still only a set of words: every child's experience is unique. It's important not to confuse your child with their diagnosis.

Children don't like to be 'different' and the risk of attaching too much significance to a label like ADHD is that they may internalize a sense that there's something wrong with them. As with any medical diagnosis, these sorts of labels can form a screen that makes it harder to see a child clearly. It's not wrong to apply such labels, but they shouldn't obscure the unique qualities each child possesses.

We all need to feel accepted, acknowledged and understood, and the most important thing is to create a space of awareness where you approach your child with an attitude of curiosity – and look beyond their symptoms to see the individual beneath.

The five key points

Be a safe haven from stress at school

- Parents can't change the system overnight, but they can make sure a child feels nurtured and heard.

- Make sure your child knows that their well-being is more important than their grades.

- Anxiety is common in classrooms: there is a lot you can do to help your child stay centred.

- Ask your child how you can best support them, especially at exam time.

- Crises will pass quicker if you can work through them calmly.

Make the online world work for your family

It's not so long since mobile phones were the stuff of science fiction. Today, a six-year-old armed with a smartphone wields more computing power than NASA marshalled to land astronauts on the moon. No previous generation of parents has been forced to confront the implications of such a profound technological shift for their 'diginatives' – the first humans to grow up surrounded by mobile devices from birth. The technology has opened up undreamed-of worlds to young people, allowing them to inform and educate themselves in ways that we would have found unimaginable, and to forge diverse friendships that span the globe.

For all these wonderful benefits, the technology is still so new that there is no consensus on what impact it may have or how best to handle it. One day we are being warned of the dangers tablets may pose to young attention spans, only for another study to suggest that computer games enhance problem-solving skills. We may wonder whether there is a 'right' age for children to start using devices and worry about the consequences of excessive screen time on maturing brains. We might also be concerned about cyber-bullying, or possible exposure to online grooming or porn. In this new territory, there are no ready-made answers and it's easy to feel others are judging the choices we make. Traditional parent–child roles are reversed as we – the adults – find ourselves struggling to keep up with tech-savvy sons and daughters vanishing down the trail into a digital forest.

Take heart: just as parents have always had to take responsibility for a child's nutrition, twenty-first-century mums and dads are learning to oversee their youngsters' digital lives. You don't have to be on top of the latest mobile apps or developments in gaming technology to be up to the task. Today's parents are fortunate enough to remember that a world existed before the advent of mobile technology, so we can see its many facets with greater perspective than the 'diginatives', who have never known life without smartphones. Our job is not to serve as digital police, but to help children use the rational, decision-making parts of their 'upstairs' brain to reflect on their relationship with technology so they can enjoy the benefits while avoiding the pitfalls. Different children will react to technology in different ways: some may be naturally adept at making their devices work for them, others more prone to falling into an addictive relationship with their screens. With no hard-and-fast rules to follow, this is especially fertile territory for consulting your 'inner parent'.

As with every parental challenge, the most important first step is to ensure that you are acting from a place of calm and stillness within yourself. Whenever a challenge arises, there is always the possibility of pausing, dropping your attention into your body and taking five deep breaths. In this session I share a number of ways of approaching digital dilemmas that have emerged through my own work with families and the insights from others who have also confronted this issue. I also look at handling specific problems – from the increasingly common phenomenon of cyber-bullying, to online porn and sexting. In all cases, several key principles apply:

- **A continuous conversation.** It's never too early to start talking about how to make the best of the online world while minimizing the risks. Conversations should ideally start as soon as your child is old enough to search the internet or use YouTube, and you can revisit these chats as often as needed. Try to strike a casual tone rather than turning the subject into a big deal, which could put your child on edge.

- **Keep an eye on the computer.** If possible, locate the computer your child uses in a central area of the home where you can keep a discreet eye on what they are doing. Familiarize yourself with privacy settings and parental controls – while remaining mindful of children's frequent aptitude for unlocking security systems and guessing passwords. It will be harder to monitor smartphone or tablet use in the same way, which is why an open dialogue is so important.

- **Manage your reaction.** Remember to pay attention to what's going on for you when your child runs into online problems. Take five deep breaths, even as you acknowledge the reality of the distress your child may be experiencing, whether it be from cyber-bullying or other forms of abuse. Offload any upset you may feel with your partner or a friend rather than in front of your child.

- **Confiscate as a last resort.** If your child fears you may take away their device, they are less likely to tell you if they run into problems online.

- **Seek solutions together.** Use any online difficulties as opportunities to help your child develop their own problem-solving skills. There are many excellent websites to help parents and children to manage their online lives which you can work through together. (Some suggestions can be found in Resources, pages 272–3.)

- **Encourage children to think before they post.** It's not easy for impulsive teens to exercise self-restraint online, but the more you can maintain a dialogue with them about the importance of considering the impact of each status update, text and photo they send, the more likely they are to employ good judgement.

- **Emphasize the positives.** Young people love the online world and they will respond if you show an interest in the positive aspects of their experience. Ask them about the connections they make with friends, the new perspectives they gain on issues, the interests they pursue and the games they enjoy.

You and your phone

I've found that before parents begin to formulate specific plans for managing their children's use of technology, they often find it helpful to consider their own relationship with their devices. If we can manage our own phone use in an optimal way, our children are far more likely to follow suit.

It's no secret that phones are beautifully addictive. How many of us find ourselves idly scrolling while waiting at the check-out or at the bus stop, or instinctively checking our email as soon as we wake up? According to some counts, the average person checks their phone 110 times a day. Certainly, I've noticed that if I've got a bit of time to myself I can easily fritter it away on my smartphone. None of us needs reminding that it's easy to spend time immersed in a phone that might have been better spent appreciating our surroundings or chatting to a friend. Nevertheless, it can be helpful to reflect a little further on what role our devices play in our lives. Here are some of the kinds of questions some parents find it helpful to explore:

- How easily can I sit still without feeling an urge to check my phone?

- Do I check my phone because I need to, or because the distraction helps take the edge off boredom or anxiety?

- I hear a tone alerting me to a new message. Do I finish what I'm doing and check it later? Or do I feel compelled to check immediately?

- When I meet up with somebody, do I place the phone on the table between us or stow it out of sight in a coat or bag?

- Does frequent phone-checking ever cause tension in my family?

- When watching any form of live event, do I often find myself recording it on my phone rather than enjoying the moment?

- When was the last time I went out without my phone?

- When was the last time I was in a different room from my phone?

- How often do I give my child my undivided attention without pausing midway through a conversation to send a text or check my phone?

- How often am I spending time with my child without my phone in my hand?

- Do I often video or take pictures of special moments with my child instead of being fully present as they happen?

As we learn to live more in the moment, we become more aware of the effect our phones may be having on us. We become more aware of the way the ping of a new text message or a notification on Facebook tugs at our attention, demanding an instant response. As we see our habitual reactions with greater clarity, we can choose to pause and decide whether we need to check the phone straight away or stay with what we're doing and leave it for later. As always, tuning in to the sensations in our body, and noticing our breath, serves to bring us back to the here and now. By focusing our attention in this way, we make space for our 'inner parent' to speak.

The pleasures and perils of social media

In the space of only a few years, it has become hard to imagine what life would be like without Facebook, Twitter and Instagram. Many parents I speak to use their Facebook page or parenting blogs as lifelines where they can draw on the support of a like-minded community whose amusing posts or reassuring comments can be an invaluable boost after a tough day. Social media can be a source of practical advice, inspiration or support, and above all can remind us that we're not alone – especially if we are looking after kids and craving some adult company. A few minutes absorbed on our favourite sites can feel like well-deserved down time.

Nevertheless, for all these benefits, some parents report that their experiences are not always entirely positive. Much as it can be rewarding to keep up to date with our friends' news, if we're feeling a little low ourselves then we might be more vulnerable to experiencing a stab of envy as we scroll through pictures of beach holidays, children's parties or meals out. It can sometimes feel as if the carefully selected images have been filtered in some mysterious way to highlight the very areas where we feel a sense of lack in our lives. Indeed, one mother sparked newspaper headlines when she wrote in desperation that Facebook would be better named 'BeatYourselfUpBook'. On the other hand, we may be such enthusiastic contributors of images and updates to our own feeds that we find it increasingly difficult to enjoy a special dinner or a walk in the park for its own sake, rather than living in constant anticipation of a deluge of comments and likes that will follow when we post documentary evidence on our wall.

We should also be aware of what exactly it is we're sharing when we post. Bear in mind that many digital photos contain what is known as 'geo-location' data that reveals exactly where a picture was taken. You can adjust the settings on a camera or camera app to reduce the amount of this hidden 'meta-data' in each photo to ensure you are not putting more information than may be wise into the public domain. It's also possible that some children may object when they eventually discover how much of their early lives has effectively been turned into public property. In this age of 'sharenting', more and more parents are starting to question the wisdom of posting so much of their children's lives online, where images and updates can form a permanent 'digital tattoo'.

If you feel you want to explore your own relationship with social media more deeply, here are some of the sorts of questions you might wish to consider:

- How much time do I spend on social media each day?

- Do I check social media first thing in the morning? Last thing at night?

- Do I use social media as a form of entertainment?

- How often do I turn to social media to soothe myself when I feel stressed?

- What kinds of feelings do I experience as I scroll through other people's updates?

- How often am I drawn into arguments on comment pages?

- When I see a notification, do I feel compelled to check it immediately?

- How much do I know about the way the images I share of my children could potentially be accessed and reproduced by strangers?

- Do I focus on body image: how my friends look? Celebrity pictures?

- Do I find myself monitoring the number of 'likes' my posts receive? Or hoping to receive more comments?

- If I post something and I get only a few 'likes', do I feel disappointed?

- Is my absorption in social media causing me to miss out on opportunities to interact with my child and partner?

These questions do not have right or wrong answers. They are merely tools for looking more closely at your relationship with social media so that you can confidently model the kind of behaviour you'd like to see reflected by your child.

Staying safe online

There was a time when parents wondered how best to broach the subject of the birds and the bees. These days, mums and dads are working out how to talk to their children about the risks they may face online. Lecturing or trying to instil fear rarely works – children are far more likely to respond to a conversation where you are curious about what they think.

All families are facing similar challenges, and you are not alone when it comes to your concerns about safety. Parents confront a real dilemma. You may want to introduce boundaries on online activity, but on the other hand you don't want to undermine your child's ability to make the most of the internet or to socialize with other children who are not subject to the same limits. We may worry about the amount of time our child spends online – but if all his friends are doing the same, will he be left out or even exposed to bullying or ridicule if we make our own rules?

Screen time – how much is too much?

Newborn babies are likely to have their first encounter with a screen when their picture is snapped shortly after they've left the womb. Many toddlers start swiping at tablets before they reach their first birthday, and young children soon learn to play games or watch clips on YouTube.

Growing numbers of studies are trying to assess the potential impact of screens on child development, but the technology is so new that it's too early to draw firm conclusions. Some researchers have questioned whether too much screen time or television may hinder a toddler's capacity to bond with adult care-givers – though what parent hasn't plonked their kids in front of a TV or iPad from time to time, just for a moment's peace, to make space for a chat with a friend or to guarantee a stress-free plane journey? That welcome respite may be what helps you to get through the day.

Managing devices can often be so hard because they seem to stimulate the reward system in the brain – meaning it's very easy for a child's 'downstairs' brain to become activated when they are suddenly deprived of their screen, which can lead to explosive results. Tablets may seem like great pacifiers for young children, but it's essential that they learn to cope without constant digital stimulation. If young children can't sit still without a screen to distract them, they won't learn to manage their emotions, leaving them more vulnerable to mood swings and tantrums as they grow up.

With parents often adopting very different approaches, it's tempting to worry that our own policy is either too lax or too harsh, and we may feel criticized no matter what we do. Part of the answer may be to focus less on arbitrary rules and more on forming a positive vision of what your family wants to get out of digital technology and the kinds of drawbacks you want to avoid. For example, you may wish to make agreements about certain times when phones are switched off to encourage family members to talk to one another – perhaps during meals, or after a certain time of day. You might all see the value of using a tablet to help pass the time on a long car journey, but agree that if there's an opportunity to play outdoors or develop face-to-face friendships, then screens should be put away.

Finding a way to oversee screen time may seem daunting, but it can also present new opportunities to forge a deeper connection. Given the lack of any established formula, this is an ideal arena to tune in to your own guidance and trust what feels right for you.

Trolls, hate sites and 'roasting'

Cyber-bullying is by far the biggest problem affecting young people online. It can take many forms: trolling with vicious posts on social media; excluding individuals from online social groups or games; pressure to send naked selfies or engage in 'sexting'; the posting of embarrassing personal details, pictures or videos; setting up 'hate sites' or digitally blanking somebody by refusing to like or comment on their status updates or photos. Girls can often be the victims, but there are also growing numbers of teenage boys subjected to 'roasting' – nasty online attacks by gangs of female peers. Sometimes this can be an extension of bullying at school, or it can be anonymous and even conducted through fake accounts. As one mother put it to me: at least in the old days bullying only took place during school hours. In the age of cyber-bullying, it can feel like there's no escape.

It may not always be obvious if your child is being subjected to cyber-bullying, though any indication that they are feeling sad or anxious while online can be a tell-tale sign. The public nature of social media can make the target feel as if a situation is rapidly spiralling out of control. As a parent, the most important thing is to monitor your own reaction before responding. However angry or upset you feel, the best thing you can do for your child is to remain calm and work with them to agree the best course of action. For example, it's important to acknowledge the depth of the hurt they may be experiencing and ensure they feel heard. Try to avoid any variation of the 'sticks and stones may break my bones but words will never hurt me' speech: for children suffering online abuse, the wounds are all too real.

As you work through the options with your child, it's worth bearing in mind that in the online world the distinction between victim and perpetrator can easily blur. Children who engage in cyber-bullying may once have been victims themselves, and vice-versa. It's often best to resist the impulse to confront culprits or their parents immediately and instead work with your child on how to respond. However, if your child is being subjected to consistent abuse or threats online it may be wise to consult school authorities or the police. Keep screenshots of offensive material, save nasty messages and bear in mind that in some cases cyber-bullying can be a crime.

Kevin: 'It's hard enough being a teenager'

'As if being a teenager isn't difficult enough, they now have every single one of their embarrassing moments posted on social media. Every argument or falling out – it's all shared so publicly. It's torturous. Sometimes I just wish I could take the kids away to a quiet, secluded island with no technology so they could play outside and enjoy these years without any hassle or threats.

'My eldest daughter, Jodie, was telling me the other day there's a girl basically bullying her on Facebook. She's been posting really nasty things about her. Some of the language is pretty revolting – they've called her a "slut" and all sorts of horrible things. As a dad, you just don't know what to do. You can't stop your kids using social media – but it's very difficult to prevent it getting out of hand.'

Onscreen friendships

For today's 'screenagers', the internet can be a great way to expand their circle of friends and learn the value of cooperation and kindness online. For children who are shy or have difficulty socializing, online connections can be genuine lifelines. Nevertheless, friendships mediated through screens bring new risks – from the ease with which bullies can single out their victims on social media, to the dangers inherent in interacting with strangers.

I have been struck by the number of parents I have seen whose distraught children have discovered that social media has amplified the effects of the fickle friendships, insecurities over appearance and bullying that have traditionally marked turbulent teenage years. It is all too easy for teenagers grappling with difficult emotions or trying to fit in to share more in their posts than might be wise. It is perhaps not surprising that the high drama unfolding over messaging apps in hours-long exchanges can make for late nights and prove far more compelling than homework. Teenagers simply don't want to miss out on what's going on, whatever the time of day. As one teenage girl confessed to me with unabashed frankness, 'It's just more fun looking at my phone than studying. I need to constantly check in with my friends to make sure they still like me, and that I'm not missing out on anything.'

Sex, selfies and self-harm

For many teenage girls, sites such as Facebook and Instagram have become arenas where they feel obliged to spend hours snapping selfies at just the right angle and manipulating the resulting images to maximum effect. They often post pictures that make them appear far more mature than they actually are. Parents may rightfully worry about the representation of women online, when so much of the media is obsessed by surgically enhanced celebrities rather than examples of inspiring, strong role models. Likewise, with the prevalence of self-harm among teenagers rising, it's increasingly easy to find fellow self-harmers online who normalize and may even encourage the behaviour – a phenomenon which many parents understandably find incomprehensible and shocking. (For more on self-harm, see Step 8 and also Resources, page 276.)

Similarly, 'sexting' and the sending of nude selfies have become increasingly common among teenagers. Most young people don't see sexting as a problem and are understandably reluctant to discuss it with adults. For parents, it's important to maintain a continuous dialogue. You can use something you're watching on TV or a film, images on a billboard glimpsed during a car journey, or a story in the news to kick-start a casual chat about sexuality. You could also mention you've been having a conversation about teenage sexting with another parent and ask your teen what they think.

Porn

It's an unpalatable reality to confront, but the fact is that virtually every child is going to stumble across porn online. Young people are naturally curious about sex, and the sheer quantity of porn on the internet means that it's only a matter of time before they find illicit images, whether intentionally or by clicking on a seemingly innocent link that redirects them to a pornographic site.

The extreme nature of many of these images means they are obviously totally inappropriate for young people, and it's important to try to establish an honest dialogue with your child about what they might encounter online. The Thinkuknow website has a wealth of age-appropriate guidance to help you with these kinds of conversations. (See page 273 for more on Thinkuknow.) It's good to emphasize that it's natural for young people to be curious, but that porn is never a realistic representation of a loving relationship, and is comprised of scenes posed by actors working in a seedy industry rife with exploitation. Reassure your child that you would prefer them to tell you if they click on something they find disturbing and that they won't be in trouble.

If you do discover your child or teen is deliberately perusing porn online, measure your reaction carefully. You may be angry and disappointed, but it's important not to shame a young person – they will be embarrassed enough as it is. Instead, try to engage them in a dialogue about the values involved in a loving and authentic intimate relationship. It's worth remembering that just as only a small minority of children suffer any form of lasting harm from alcohol or drugs, the same holds true for porn.

Video games

There is a wealth of research on the impact of video games on children, but it can be very hard to find experts speaking with a single voice. The key question is what impact games seem to be having on *your* child. If long hours spent on an Xbox seem to plunge them into a trance-like state that leaves them restless and agitated, or triggers a meltdown when they are told to switch off, then it may be time to have a conversation about agreeing some limits. Help your child tune in to their body. How do they feel when they stop playing? Are they tense? Is their heart beating faster? Do they feel irritable or upset? Encourage them to rate themselves on the kind of 'anger thermometer' discussed in Step 7. You can work with your child to help them learn to manage their own emotions as you work together to agree boundaries.

Surveillance or trust?

Technology has brought the tension society faces between the values of personal freedom and the promise of security from a 'Big Brother'-style state into our homes. There are now growing numbers of apps and other devices that can be used to monitor or restrict a child's online activity. There is no doubt that some form of parental control is essential to keep youngsters safe online. However, the ultimate insurance policy is a HEART-centred connection with your child that will encourage them to listen to you and have the confidence to confide in you if things go wrong. Relying too heavily on technological fixes as opposed to honest conversations can send a tacit message that you don't trust them. It's far better to nurture a relationship of mutual respect. (For more resources, see pages 272–3.)

Connecting across a console

Though you might not have much interest in games, you can have a go at using them as an opportunity to connect by asking your child to show you how to play, even for a few minutes. Your predictably abysmal performance will be a guaranteed source of amusement. At a deeper level, children enjoy any situation of role reversal where they gain temporary, safe power over adults: part of the reason young kids love hide-and-seek so much is that it places them in a temporary position of dominance as they hunt down a helpless parent who is only nominally 'hidden'. Similarly, computer games can elevate your child into a position of authority and cast you in the role of apprentice.

Here are some more suggestions for ways in which you can use technology to connect:

- **Rite of passage.** Entrusting a child with a phone or other device can be seen as an important initiation – one that can help them develop a sense of responsibility and mark their growing independence. It can be a good moment to have a fresh conversation about avoiding risks online and maximizing benefits.

- **Shared experience.** Brothers and sisters who might be prone to arguing can often set their differences aside through a shared session on a two-player game, especially when it involves standing shoulder-to-shoulder fighting off a horde of extra-terrestrials, or saving civilization from a zombie apocalypse.

- **Online etiquette.** Parents can encourage children to use the unique opportunities for meeting new people offered by the internet to practise the qualities of kindness, generosity, fairness and respect they would show to people they meet in person.

- **Crisis as opportunity.** As in any situation where a child is struggling, whether it be from the fall-out from cyber-bullying or losing sleep to the lure of the Xbox, the crisis can provide an opportunity to help a child develop a 'growth mindset' and learn to find answers for themselves.

- **Find your tribe.** Parents differ widely in their approaches to screens and the online world. Team up with friends who share a similar philosophy so that you can support each other's efforts to set appropriate limits and exchange ideas on what works.

Making contracts

One option for helping your children and teenagers to learn to make technology work for them is to create a formal 'contract' governing their – and your – screen time.

The idea is to sit down with them and come up with a set of agreements on the kind of boundaries that the whole family will apply to the use of devices. This sort of democratic approach allows you to demonstrate what it means to make an agreement and be accountable for your behaviour. Contracts might cover issues such as:

- The amount of time allocated to TV/playing video games/using a tablet per day.

- A 'switch off' time for devices in the evening.

- Dedicated 'digital detox' periods when everyone agrees to take a break from their devices.

- No scrolling through phones at mealtimes.

- Commitments by all the family on the parameters for their individual screen use.

- Possible consequences if the contract is not respected.

This contract can then be typed up, signed and posted on a wall. (There are a number of templates for such contracts available online – see pages 272–3.)

The advantage of such contracts is that they provide opportunities for discussion and a sense of shared commitment to making the most of technology while mitigating the downsides. As a parent, the exercise provides a chance to model the skills of empathy and discernment – guiding your children with confidence while giving them their say in a family decision. Having an explicit contract can also provide a sense of 'containment', helping both parents and children manage their concerns around devices. The process of setting the contract also allows parents to learn from their children about the way they use phone apps, games or tablets. A child feels respected and heard, while parents become more familiar with the reality of their online life.

Contracts can also help foster a sense of responsibility and accountability. For example, what would be the consequences if a phone is lost or broken – will the cost have to be reimbursed, perhaps in a token form through some set number of hours of chores? For older children, working through the real-world rules of signing contracts with a phone company may be a safe way to start introducing them to adult financial responsibilities.

Children who sign these contracts will often attempt to push the boundaries, as they will with any rule. This can be seen as part of a healthy impulse on the part of a child to explore and test the world around them. The fact you have taken the trouble to reach an agreement set down in the contract should make it easier for you to insist the rules are respected. It's important to talk through any breach to provide your child with an opportunity to problem-solve. The message parents are sending is, 'I'm here, we can get through this – let's work out how we're going to deal with it.' Ask your child the question, 'What can we do to help you to avoid doing that again in the future?'

Working through all this with kindness

The many dilemmas posed by technology mean that there are bound to be times when it is impossible to live up to the commitments that you may have made. In such situations, it's easy to begin to catastrophize over the potential impact of too much screen time, or the risks your child may be facing online. Meet these moments with gentleness and kindness for yourself, rather than finding another excuse to let your 'inner critic' off the leash. These are new challenges; we are all finding our way through them – and ultimately there is no hard-and-fast right or wrong way. It can help to remember to say to yourself: 'I am kind to myself in this moment, and I am kind to my child.'

The five key points

Make the online world work for your family

- Helping a child manage technology is an essential part of modern parenting.

- Explore your own relationship with your phone to set the right example.

- Kids react differently to screens: trust your judgement on what's right.

- Educate yourself and start the conversation on screen use early.

- Work collaboratively through family meetings or by making contracts.

Step
10

Learn to be kind
to yourself

There are now enough studies demonstrating the positive impact of kindness on our physical and emotional well-being to collapse a bookshelf. The effects are so powerful that some psychologists believe that kindness should rank alongside a balanced diet, regular exercise and quitting smoking as among the basic steps we might take to improve our health. According to Richard Davidson, an American neuroscientist who has spent many years studying compassion, feelings of kindness and generosity sustain positive emotion in the brain more than anything else yet measured in his field. Our heart rate slows, we secrete the 'bonding hormone' oxytocin, and more blood is pumped through the parts of the brain linked to empathy, care-giving and feelings of pleasure. The benefits include:

- Greater ability to handle stress

- Healthier functioning of the heart

- Lasting increase in happiness levels

- Less mind-wandering and immersion in negative thoughts

- Better relationships

Despite all the wonderful benefits, I often find that with parents I must approach the K-word with extreme caution – and only with careful preparation. However innocent the idea of being a bit nicer to ourselves may sound, it can be very hard to give ourselves permission to put this into practice. The mere mention of self-kindness can trigger these kinds of reactions:

- 'Sounds very unnatural to me.'

- 'Don't be ridiculous – I can't change my personality.'

- 'It sounds selfish.'

- 'I don't have time!'

- 'That's all very well, but I need to put my children first.'

Every mum and dad I see is doing the best they can and wants nothing but the best for their children. Nevertheless, we often speak to ourselves in far harsher tones than we would ever use to a friend who is struggling, and our schedules may rarely feature time to do something just for ourselves. We all seem to suffer from this drought of self-compassion to a certain extent, and I frequently discover that this is one of the most rewarding issues to explore when working with parents. It can be surprisingly difficult to persuade mums and dads to show themselves more kindness, but it can yield huge dividends for them and their families.

In this final step, we look at why cultivating a more compassionate attitude towards ourselves is such a good idea, why it can seem so difficult, and the sorts of small, manageable steps we can take to bring more of this magical quality into our daily lives. There's nothing selfish about this process: as we learn to take better care of ourselves, we have a natural tendency to find new ways to care for others, especially our children.

Kindness Is Good for Our Health

In purely physical terms, compassion is so good for us in part because it stimulates the Vagus nerve – the 'brake' on the nervous system we activate by taking deep, full-bellied breaths, which we encountered in Step 1 (see pages 5–8). Having a healthy 'Vagal tone' is linked to the efficient

Continued . . .

functioning of the heart, so practising kindness can reduce the risk of heart disease. The Vagus nerve also affects how we relate to other people: it's linked to nerves that tune our ears to speech, coordinate eye contact and regulate emotional expressions. So, along with taking five deep breaths, practising compassion is a great way to keep your Vagus nerve healthy and tune in to the wisdom of your brain, heart and gut – a topic we discussed in more depth in Step 3.

Why is being kind to ourselves so hard?

We have talked about the way the 'frenemy' in our head generates a constant stream of thinking: often comprised largely of fears about the future and regrets about the past. Many parents find that in all this incessant chatter, one voice tends to dominate – the harsh tones of a vocal 'inner critic' who is ever eager to dwell on the negatives and tell us exactly where we're going wrong (often when we're trying to fall asleep, or when we wake up in the small hours before the alarm).

We may assume that this voice is helping to motivate us, and tell ourselves that we won't achieve much if we start cutting ourselves too much slack. In reality, the 'inner critic' is putting us down and draining us of the energy we need to tackle our day. We'd get far more done if we spoke to ourselves with words of encouragement rather than criticism, but we're so used to listening to our 'inner critic' that we may never question whether it's really telling us the truth. Even people who are enjoying life and thriving as parents can be plagued by a voice warning that it could all fall apart at any moment – a sneaking suspicion that things are 'too good to last'.

The seductive dangers of comparison

Since the earliest days of our caveman ancestors, human beings have been social creatures with a powerful urge to connect. Parents naturally look to others for ideas and inspiration – and for a sense of belonging to a wider community. As soon as our children are born, we want to know how they are doing in relation to their peers and that they are passing the right milestones at the right times. It can be very helpful to compare notes with other parents as part of a supportive community, but if we spend too much time focusing on what others are doing, it's easy to start questioning whether we're doing a good enough job.

Social media – despite its many benefits – has turned our natural inclination to compare into an epidemic. Now we're only a click away from somebody who seems to be more accomplished, better looking, wealthier or handling their family life in an enviably relaxed and successful style (often in a picture-postcard setting). Even if we realize at some level that the images we see are carefully filtered, and the lives of our friends may be messier than their status updates or Instagram feeds suggest, the niggling feeling of inferiority can burrow into our minds like a worm.

Such feelings are perfect food for the 'inner critic'. Expert at kicking us when we're down, this voice has an uncanny habit of striking when we least expect. The 'inner critic' loves to compare us unfavourably with others and is constantly finding new targets: whether it be an impeccably attired mum at the school gate, a dad who seems to have it all together, or a celebrity model whose body's back in shape six weeks after having a baby. Even if we succeed in temporarily silencing the voice in one area of our lives, it always seems to pop up in another. Our 'inner critic' knows all our weak spots and is even more difficult to ignore when we're feeling sensitive, tired or vulnerable.

It's not selfish to be kind to yourself

After so many years of being hard on ourselves, practising kindness is not easy. Many of us grew up in households run by parents who found it hard to be kind to themselves, and we may have inherited their self-critical stance without even realizing it, unknowingly depriving ourselves of one of our most valuable resources. We might have learned the lesson early on that putting our own needs first is necessarily selfish in some way – and we may feel this even more strongly when we have children of our own.

There is still an unspoken assumption in our society

that parents should sacrifice everything for their children. But being kind to yourself does not mean being neglectful of your children, selfish, self-indulgent or self- absorbed. It's the precise opposite of wallowing in self-pity. The aim is to take the constructive step of thinking for a moment about how you might be able to comfort and care for yourself at any given time. Nevertheless, mums and dads who do make an occasional attempt to put their own needs first often feel torn: 'It's all very well trying to look after myself, but where's the time?'

I learned the value of self-kindness myself a few years ago when I was going through a particularly tough time. Looking back, I can see I was grieving over the deaths of several loved ones and the break-up of a long-term relationship. But instead of facing my feelings, I spent two years numbing myself with stodgy takeaways, alcohol, partying and flings. As I slowly began to realize, all this running away wasn't the answer and certainly wouldn't make me happy in the long run.

Being kinder to ourselves takes courage. We start to deepen our appreciation of the simple but often forgotten truth that being imperfect, making mistakes and experiencing difficulties are an inevitable part of being a parent. Our vulnerability is nothing to be ashamed of. In fact, facing the tender spots within ourselves helps us to connect with others more deeply, including our children.

Needed: a subtle but profound shift

The irony is that parents tend to be experts at showing kindness to others, but helping them direct some of this kindness inwards is one of the most difficult parts of my job. Some feel angry if I even imply that they might consider showing themselves more compassion, because if it were that simple, they would have done it already. At times, even mentioning the K-word can temporarily make things worse – prompting yet another outburst from the 'inner critic' who is always on stand-by to point out that previous attempts at self-compassion have ended in dismal failure. Everyone knows that work–life balance is important, but self-care can turn into just another out-of-reach target and another reason to feel like we're failing. How many of us think we're getting it right?

Though I often have to put this very diplomatically – sometimes after many sessions of offering reassurance – the reality in many families is that a lack of self-compassion is not only a question of time. Finding space to show ourselves more kindness is about a subtle but profound shift in perspective. We have to make a conscious decision to be nicer to ourselves. We can then see kindness as a skill to practise, albeit one that we may not have learned much about in childhood, and certainly weren't taught in school.

Learning to be kinder to yourself is not something that happens in a flash. Like any habit, it can be cultivated through small, regular steps. It's all about learning to recognize when the 'inner critic' has seized the controls. It would be futile to try to silence this voice permanently and probably not a very good idea: just like other parts of ourselves, it has its unique part to play. But there's no point giving the 'inner critic' more air time than it deserves. Even noticing when it has begun running its old routines immediately starts to weaken its hold.

Your secret superpower: setting intentions

While the mind can often behave like a troublesome 'frenemy', it can also be an incredibly powerful force for generating feelings of well-being – when we remember to take charge. But as we all know, changing long-standing patterns of behaviour can take time. Just as our New Year's resolutions to get to the gym more often or eat healthier food can fall by the wayside, so our commitment to be kinder to ourselves can be hard to maintain. It's worth persevering: bringing more kindness into your life can change your whole experience of parenting for the better.

I have found that one of the most powerful techniques for enlisting the help of the mind – rather than constantly fighting it – is to set an intention: a clear statement of a particular way you want to be in the world. You can then return to this intention whenever you notice your commitment to yourself has started to slip. I find the technique works best if you use an 'I am' statement, for example:

- I am being kinder to myself.

- I am cultivating compassionate thoughts.

- I am finding time to focus on feelings of kindness and compassion.

The key with intention-setting is to really experience the feeling associated with the 'I am' statement as you make it. For example, if your intention is to be kinder to yourself, take a moment to think of a person or animal you care about. Breathe the feeling of kindness into your heart area. Really try to experience the feeling you want to bring into your life as you repeat the intention. This may feel a little strange at first, but deliberately generating feelings in this way will serve to anchor your new way of being in your body, as well as your mind.

You can practise this as many times as you wish. Parents I work with often find it helpful to write their intentions down. You can use a notebook or write them on postcards and stick them up in a place where you will see them every day, such as on the fridge or on a wardrobe door. You can begin this practice at any time – though it's also wonderful to take some time to set clear intentions at the start of a new year or on your birthday.

Try not to get too attached to exactly *how* your intention will come about. The important thing is to keep cultivating the feeling associated with your new commitment to yourself. When you review your intentions a year later, you may be surprised at how much has changed.

Starting small: planting new thoughts

As with the cultivation of any new habit, the key with kindness is to start small. You don't have to take radical action: begin by reflecting a little on the sorts of thoughts you want to encourage. Like flowers being watered, the more attention you give to them, the more they will thrive.

When I was working through my own difficult times, I found it very helpful to write kind phrases to myself over and over again in my journal. I would repeat them every evening and then I would read them back to myself on the bus to work. I'd also look out for inspiring quotes online or in magazines, and I'd make a note of anything or anyone who inspired me or helped me feel better. Our feelings of unworthiness can be like onions – just when you feel you're getting somewhere, you find another layer. I found that repeating these kind phrases was a powerful way to begin gradually and gently peeling more of those layers away.

Some parents find it helpful to memorize a set of kind phrases they can repeat silently when they feel upset. Though they may jar at first, saying, writing or reading such statements on a regular basis will generate powerful feelings of self-compassion in the long run. Here are some possibilities:

- This is really difficult for me right now.

- Everyone feels this way sometimes.

- May I be kind to myself in this moment.

- I am worthy of giving myself some care.

- It's all okay really.

- You are doing all right.

- Nobody is perfect.

- Just breathe.

- I value myself.

- I am enough.

- Life feels relentless right now and I deserve a break.

- I deserve to be taken care of just as much as the rest of my family.

- I allow myself time to step back and look after myself.

- I work through my difficult feelings at my own pace.

- We are all in this together.

Cues to be kind

As you begin to weave such phrases into your daily life, it can be helpful to give yourself a little nudge to remember them at regular intervals. Here are some possible cues:

- Carry an **object** that reminds you to be kind to yourself, such as a special stone or pendant. Or perhaps a memento from someone you love.

- Stick **Post-it notes** with inspiring quotes or kind phrases around the house. You could put them on the fridge, by the bed, by the kettle, or make notes on your phone or in your journal. Or use a **white board** with coloured pens.

- Select a **cue moment** to rehearse one of the quotes. It could be just before you sit down to eat, before you read your child a story or every time you close the front door.

Me time

Repeating kind phrases is a powerful practice – but seemingly small *acts* of kindness to oneself can make an even bigger difference. Raising the next generation is the most important job anyone can do: value yourself enough to make sure you sometimes do things that you enjoy. The very act of making a conscious decision to show yourself some compassion in the way you might to a child, friend or animal can make a big difference to how you feel. Here are some suggestions:

- Phone or text a friend you have been meaning to contact for ages and organize a catch-up.

- Buy yourself a treat, such as flowers, chocolates or a magazine.

- Go for a walk, get some fresh air or do some gardening.

- Take a long bubble bath, inhaling the fragrances.

- Walk barefoot on grass or soil.

- Take five deep breaths.

- Linger over a cup of tea or your favourite coffee.

- Come up with some inspiring songs on Spotify or iTunes that reflect kindness. Share playlists with your friends or family.

- Watch something that used to make you laugh – live comedy is great, but clips on YouTube are also a wonderful way to reconnect with that lighter part of yourself.

- Put your hands over your heart or give yourself a hug – something you can do in private if you feel self-conscious. These gestures can be surprisingly powerful and can help us get out of our busy chattering minds and into our bodies.

● Some parents make a 'Kindness Wall' where family members make a note of kind acts they have performed or received during the week – a great way to share the benefits.

● Finally, meditation can be really helpful and there is strong evidence for its benefits. There are many forms – from simple ways to become more self-aware to more formal periods of sitting quietly, practising yoga or walking mindfully in nature. (See Resources, pages 263–5 and 278–9.)

Such steps will not only help you to foster greater compassion for yourself – you will also be modelling self-care for your children.

Rosemary: 'It was about giving myself permission'

'I like swimming, I know it's good for me and I know all its benefits – but I'd stopped going. My friend told me that I don't value myself enough to make it a priority. I'm juggling so much – making sure my kids get to their after-school clubs, tidying up after others, organizing shopping

Continued . . .

> *or meals – and it slips off the agenda. But going back felt amazing. It was about giving myself permission to spend this time on me. Now it's part of my routine and I know it's good for me.'*

Sending kindness into the world

The wonderful thing about compassion is that it works in all directions – like a miniature sun that lights everything touched by its rays. Self-compassion cannot help but inspire feelings of expansiveness and generosity: as you start to go easier on yourself, you'll naturally find yourself feeling kinder towards others. It can be a powerful practice to make a more conscious effort to foster this kind of altruism beyond your immediate circle, even if you only take baby steps. We've all experienced how even the briefest of smiles or a moment of authentic connection with a stranger can brighten your and someone else's day, but it's easy to miss such chances when our schedules feel so crammed. Nevertheless, it's good to remember that at the deepest level we are all connected – and every act of kindness makes a difference.

Matthieu Ricard is a Buddhist monk who has been dubbed the 'world's happiest man' after brain-imaging studies suggested he possessed almost supernatural reserves of tranquillity. He has recommended spending ten seconds silently wishing happiness on strangers you pass in the street or sit next to on the bus. The positive effects on your own mind linger for some time after you have chosen these kind thoughts. Ricard compares the afterglow to the scent that lingers after you briefly open a bottle of perfume.

Cultivating compassion is not about seeking approval or some kind of reward from others. Family or friends might not comment on or even seem to notice your new perspective – and that doesn't matter. The important thing is to pay attention to how *you* feel as you consciously practise being kinder to yourself and others.

The wonderful thing about kindness is that it has such a strong ripple effect. This principle was beautifully illustrated by a teacher at a south-east London primary school who organized pupils to attach handwritten, uplifting notes to copies of the *Metro* newspaper. Some of the readers were so moved that they wrote letters of appreciation, which in turn multiplied the feelings of goodwill. This was only one aspect of a much wider Kindness Project in Schools, initiated by Action for Happiness, an organization aiming to promote a kinder society, in collaboration with Bernadette Russell, author of *Do Nice, Be Kind, Spread Happy*, a book about acts of kindness for children. Here are some other recent examples of kind acts by strangers in Britain that had such a big impact on individuals that they made the news:

- In January 2015, a man on a train to Bristol handed a young mother with a three-year-old £5 for a drink and a handwritten note calling her a 'credit to your generation' and praising her parenting skills. The twenty-three-year-old mother said her anonymous benefactor's generosity had made her want to cry.

● In December 2015, a seven-year-old boy from Aberdeen asked his friends and family to donate food to a local food bank rather than give him any birthday presents since he felt sad about people who could not afford meals and he had enough toys. His mum said he was 'chuffed' with the 70kg-pile of goods he was able to donate.

● In May 2016, a mother went on Facebook to thank a member of staff at a supermarket in Basingstoke who had helped her with her young daughters who were having a meltdown at the check-out. The woman lightened the mood by allowing one of the girls – both of whom are registered as blind and have autism – to help scan the items. 'This very kind lady decided to help instead of judge,' the mother posted. 'It melts my heart to come across people that are prepared to go the extra mile – and little acts of kindness make a massive difference to my world.' Her post gained half a million 'likes'.

While these kinds of striking stories illustrate the enormous power of kindness, it is arguably the little-noticed, consistent, everyday actions that have an even more profound impact. It can be the simplest of gestures – such as stopping to chat to a lonely-looking mum in the playground – that can make all the difference.

Hannah: 'I did the best I could to reassure her'

'I started chatting in the playground to Kate, another mum, who looked really stressed and upset. Kate opened up to me and told me it had been the fifth morning in a row that her eight-year-old had shouted and screamed at her and she couldn't get him to sit down and eat breakfast or get dressed. Kate is tired, blames herself and takes her son's words and behaviour personally. I did the best I could to reassure her and I think it gave her a little lift. Taking a moment to do this made me feel good too.'

Gratitude: compassion's transformative twin

We probably all have a childhood memory of being told to 'count our blessings'. The phrase arguably ranks alongside 'worse things happen at sea' or 'there's no point crying over spilt milk' in the top ten irritating clichés that only make us feel worse. Come to think of it, 'When life hands you lemons, make lemonade' is also a strong contender.

However, it would be a mistake to dismiss the profound power of gratitude. Just as neuroscientists have confirmed what sages always knew when it comes to kindness, the results of studies into gratitude have been equally striking. Pioneering research in this relatively new field has shown the many benefits that taking a moment to be thankful can have for our bodies and minds, including:

- more optimism, happiness and joy

- stronger immune systems and lower blood pressure

- fewer feelings of loneliness and isolation

- acting with greater generosity and compassion

- fewer symptoms of depression

The good news is that you don't even need to identify anything in particular to be grateful for. The very act of trying to think about something good in your life encourages your brain to secrete the feel-good neurotransmitter serotonin (the active ingredient in a number of commonly prescribed antidepressants). With a little practice, you can quickly establish a virtuous cycle in which the brain starts automatically to scan for more and more reasons to be grateful. Some of the parents I work with are surprised at how much better they feel when they actively start to appreciate the little things in life – such as meeting up with a friend for a coffee or sharing a joke with their child. Taking a moment to appreciate what you already have – rather than focusing on what you feel is missing – can provide a real lift, especially on bad days when you're stressed and tired.

As with compassion, gratitude is a wonderful habit to nurture. Here are some tips to bring more of this quality into your daily life:

- **Gratitude diary.** Make it a habit to jot down in your journal a few things that have gone well that day. You need only do this two or three times a week. As you write, dwell on the positive feelings you experience. The more detail you can include as to why you are grateful for each entry, the better.

- **Rituals.** Perform little rituals to remind you to focus on the positives. For example, before eating dinner, each member of the family could take a turn to identify something they are happy about. Or you could create a 'gratitude jar', with each family member putting in a marble each day to represent something good that's happened. Children love these kinds of games as they give them a glimpse into their parents' world.

- **Gratitude 'first aid kit'.** If something triggers old, negative feelings, or puts your 'frenemy' mind into overdrive, it can be helpful to shift your mood by thinking about the many things that have gone well in the past.

- **Thank-you notes.** The habit of writing thank-you notes may have gone out of fashion in the digital age, but writing short notes to somebody who has been helpful, or in return for a gift, is a powerful way to express gratitude.

- **Delivering a 'gratitude letter'.** Write a detailed letter to a relative, friend or mentor – someone who has inspired, helped or supported you. Deliver the letter in person and you may feel the most intense wave of gratitude you have ever experienced. The recipient is almost certain to be profoundly moved by such a special gesture.

- **Gratitude apps.** There are a number of excellent gratitude apps designed to help parents identify the good things that have happened each day. (See Resources, pages 282–4).

Giving yourself permission

Starting consciously to bring more kindness and gratitude into your daily life through thoughts and actions is an excellent practice. If this works for you, you might consider taking a further step by exploring ways to carve out a little more time for yourself in the course of a busy week.

This can be particularly helpful if you are feeling that it's a struggle to adjust to the inevitably big changes that becoming a parent involves. These can affect people in many different ways. Some mourn the loss of their independence, while others eagerly embrace a whole new perspective on life – with many parents somewhere in between, struggling to find a balance.

The question isn't really whether you have lost or gained, but how you feel about yourself right now and whether you believe you are embodying the values you want to stand for in your life today. Amid all the pressures of parenting, it can make a huge difference if you can give yourself permission to set aside even a small amount of time to do something that 'lights you up' in some way – perhaps an activity you used to enjoy but have given up since you started work, got married or had children.

Here are some techniques I use with mums and dads to help them reconnect with the parts of themselves beyond their role as parents:

- Find a simple outlet for expressing creativity without feeling any need to perform or impress. For example, you could draw, enjoy a mindful colouring book, make music, sing, dance, write, take photographs, sew, knit, make pottery, arrange flowers or paint. Allowing yourself to become absorbed in any form of creative activity is one of the most powerful ways to focus your mind on something different, and can leave you feeling inspired and refreshed.

● Create a weekly ritual that allows you to spend some time alone. Sticking as far as possible to the same day and time will help make this into a habit.

● Ask yourself: 'What change can I embrace right now to make me happier?' Whether the change is at home, at work, finding a new hobby or volunteering, your next step is to take action.

● Identify goals beyond your role as parent. These could range from plans to study or start a business to completing a 5k run or joining a book club.

● There may be ways to find time to enjoy doing something that you did before the children arrived – even if you can only manage to do it for a short time. Possibilities might include:

- Playing a sport/hiking/rock-climbing or adventure sports
- Joining a choir or kirtan chanting group
- Exercise classes – yoga, Pilates, Zumba or gym
- Gardening or taking walks in nature
- A spa day with friends
- Cinema or theatre trips
- Connecting with spiritual communities

- Cake-baking groups or other shared activities for parents
- Joining supportive online parenting communities

Arranging such activities might sound like a big ask – after all, if it were easy to take these kinds of breaks, every parent would be doing it. It doesn't matter if your plans sometimes get cancelled at the last minute or have to be changed: the important thing is gradually to shift your mindset by recognizing that making a little time for yourself is a vital part of parenting, and your whole family will benefit.

Lisa: 'I just want a bit of "me" back'

'I know I'm exhausted. I know I have a tendency to look on the gloomy side of life. I think maybe that partly came from my mum – she was always critical of my boyfriends and she placed a really high value on looks. My dad was quite strict, almost like one of those Victorian dads. He never expressed his feelings, and I never really had much confidence. I know I blame myself for my fifteen-year-old Emily's problems, but I can't see how I can stop that. I can't help it. It's just the way I am.'

Continued . . .

When I asked Lisa where the fun was in her life, she looked at me and cried, *'I don't have fun any more. I just want a bit of "me" back.'*

I worked with Lisa to find some phrases that spoke to her, even though at first they felt a little awkward. She came up with the following affirmations and saved them on her phone:

● *You're only human. I know you're feeling really stressed right now, but this will pass.*

● *This feeling is only temporary.*

● *Things can get better, and they have got better. Just take it day by day.*

● *You've got some really nice things to look forward to.*

As we explored her feelings more deeply, Lisa began to see that it would be okay for her to take a break. It wasn't just her busy schedule that was holding her back, but her false belief that showing herself some kindness would undermine her performance as a mum.

We worked out a few things that wouldn't take too much time that she would enjoy – including an evening reconnecting with girlfriends. Lisa had done an art degree and once enjoyed painting. One Sunday, she gave herself an hour to get her easel out of the loft and have a go at painting again. Her face came alive as she described the feeling of rediscovering the neglected, creative part of herself.

'It felt so good to be doing something artistic again. Hours passed and it just took my mind off all the stressful things that had been happening. I've noticed that when I'm more relaxed, Emily's also a little better and is taking a bit more responsibility. This kindness practice is a new thing for me and I'm helping Emily learn to do it for herself as well. It feels good to laugh again.'

The five key points

Learn to be kind to yourself

- Science shows that kindness is good for your body and brain.

- It's not selfish to give yourself a break: your kids will benefit.

- Setting intentions is your secret superpower.

- Make kindness a habit: every small action makes a difference.

- Gratitude for simple things is an instant mood-lifter.

Afterword

Being a parent is hard. We aspire to do the best we can in every moment, but there will be times when we feel disappointment, a sense of failure or regret. These feelings are inevitable. Indeed, we are all conditioned to respond to challenges in the present by what happened in our past. We may make a sincere effort to change, only to discover that our habitual ways of thinking and behaving have enormous momentum. Slipping once again into an old pattern of self-blame, we can lose hope that we'll ever be able to approach life differently. This is true of every human being. The struggles we face as individuals are merely aspects of a collective, planetary predicament reflected in the many crises facing humanity as a whole.

My goal in writing this book was to invite you to consider a simple proposition: you are more powerful than you think. We don't need to be perfect parents to make an impact in our own lives – and the lives of others. Each time we manage to step back for a moment from our 'frenemy' mind counts for more than we might assume. Each time we manage to show ourselves and others a little more kindness and compassion, we send a positive ripple through the living web that connects us all. Each time we can take a moment to truly listen strengthens our HEART-centred connection with our daughter, son, or partner. Every child who feels supported, nurtured and understood – and every mum and dad who feels a little more confident – is like another bulb lighting up.

If you have read this far then the chances are that you have already begun to sense the kind of shift in perspective that taking a step back from your busy life can offer. As we start to practise in whatever way feels right for us, we begin to see the effects accumulate over time. It's as if a new dimension has opened in our lives – one where we have more choice over how we think and feel than we had imagined possible. Some of the pointers or stories in this book may speak to you more directly than others, but I emphasize that *Happy Parent, Happy Child* is intended merely as a gateway, and I encourage you to explore further for yourself. There are some suggestions for books, groups and organizations I have found helpful on my own journeys with parents in the following pages, but there is no set path. Give yourself permission to make a little time to read more widely in this field or try a new workshop or course. Or simply reach out to others. Share your experiences, and understand that you are not alone in your struggle for greater balance and harmony. These are simple steps but you may be surprised at where they lead.

A great deal is written these days in the media about the mental health 'crisis' gripping our current generation of teens – and the growing numbers of children also seeking help. There is no doubt that this should be a source of grave concern for everybody who cares about the future of this country. But there is another side to this story. Every day in my work with children and teenagers, I am struck by how much more willing they are to open up and explore their thoughts and feelings than I was at their age. The courage shown by so many young people in seeking to confront and resolve their difficult emotions – rather than suppress or numb them – should be an inspiration to us all. While doing our best to support our sons and daughters, we should always remember that they have much to teach.

Nevertheless, the real sense of distress and being overwhelmed that so many families are experiencing is a clear sign that things need to change. Just as life has a habit of giving us the sometimes challenging lessons we need to learn as individuals to develop our highest potential, so it seems our society has arrived at a point where we need fundamentally to rethink the system we use to educate our children and mitigate some of the unnecessary stress it causes to pupils, parents and teachers. I have no doubt that there is an archetypal 'inner parent' watching over our country – and she is willing us to begin this endeavour as a matter of urgency. As individuals, it's easy to feel powerless, but let's not forget that every one of our thoughts, words and deeds reverberates in space and time in ways we can never fully perceive. Every kind act, every deep breath and every mindful pause counts.

AFTERWORD

If this book can encourage a few mums and dads to trust their intuition a little more often and go a bit easier on themselves then it will have fulfilled its purpose. But my sincere hope is that as these small steps multiply, their impact will spread beyond individual families and gradually foster the kinds of changes we need to see in society as a whole, and in particular in our classrooms. As more of us place our faith in our 'inner parent', the more chance we'll have of coming together to create schools that place as much emphasis on cultivating resilience, creativity and compassion as they do on exam results, and where emotional intelligence, love of nature and well-being are prized as much as academic excellence. We'll need to listen to our hearts as well as our heads if we're going to succeed in the most important task facing Britain today: raising a generation of happier, healthier kids who aren't programmed to conform, but who are brimming with enthusiasm for building a society fit for all our futures.

References

Step 1

page 5 Vagus nerve: Bergland, Christopher, 'The neuro-biology of grace under pressure', *Psychology Today*, 2 February 2013

page 5 Bergland, Christopher, 'How does the vagus nerve convey gut instincts to the brain?', *Psychology Today*, 23 May 2014

page 5 Cuda, Gretchen, 'Just breathe: Body has a built-in stress reliever', *NPR*, 6 December 2010

Step 2

page 18 Observer mind: Tolle, Eckhart, *The Power of Now: A Guide to Spiritual Enlightenment*, London: Yellow Kite, 2001

page 19 Thinking traps: Beck, Aaron, *Depression: Clinical, Experimental, and Theoretical Aspects*, New York: Harper & Row, 1967

—— Burns, David, *The Feeling Good Handbook*, New York: William Morrow and Company, 1989

REFERENCES

Step 3

page 36 History of parenting: Watson, John, *Psychological Care of Infant and Child*, New York: W. W. Norton, 1928

—— Spock, Benjamin, *The Common Sense Book of Baby and Child Care*, New York: Duell, Sloan and Pearce, 1946

page 37 Origins of attachment research: Bowlby, John, 'The Nature of the Child's Tie to His Mother', *International Journal of Psycho-Analysis*, 1958

—— Bowlby, John, 'Separation Anxiety', *International Journal of Psycho-Analysis*, 1959

page 42 HeartMath Institute in California: www.heartmath.com

Step 4

page 67 Staying Connected: Neufeld, Gordon, and Maté, Gabor, *Hold on to Your Kids: Why Parents Need to Matter More Than Peers*, New York: Ballantine Books, 2006

page 73 Active listening: Rogers, Carl, and Evans Farson, Richard, *Active Listening*, Chicago: University of Chicago Industrial Relations Center, 1957

page 82 Power animals: Schwarz, Lisa, et al., *The Comprehensive Resource Model: Effective Therapeutic Techniques for the Healing of Complex Trauma (Explorations in Mental Health)*, London: Routledge, 2016

page 84 Role of mentors: Biddulph, Steve, *Raising Boys: Why Boys Are Different – and How to Help Them Become Happy and Well-Balanced Men*, Warriewood, NSW: Finch Publishing, 1997

Step 5

page 99 Single word reminders: Faber, Adele and Mazlish, Elaine, *How to Talk So Teens Will Listen and Listen So Teens Will Talk*, London: Piccadilly Press, 2006

page 105 Dry-eyed syndrome: Stiffelman, Susan, *Parenting Without Power Struggles: Raising Joyful, Resilient Kids While Staying Cool, Calm, and Connected*, New York: Morgan James Publishing, 2009

Step 6

page 110 Building resilience: Neufeld, Gordon, and Maté, Gabor, *Hold on to Your Kids: Why Parents Need to Matter More Than Peers*, New York: Ballantine Books, 2006

page 113 Growth mindset: Dweck, Carol, *Mindset: How You Can Fulfil Your Potential*, London: Robinson, 2012

Step 7

page 128 'Upstairs' and 'downstairs' brain/'flipping your lid': Siegel, Daniel, and Payne Bryson, Tina, *The Whole-Brain Child: 12 Revolutionary Strategies to Nurture Your Child's Developing Mind*, New York: Random House Publishing Group, 2011

page 129 'Neural wi-fi': Goleman, Daniel, *Social Intelligence: The New Science of Human Relationships*, New York: Arrow, 2007

page 133 MindUP™: The Hawn Foundation. *The MindUP curriculum.*

REFERENCES

page 136 Tend and befriend: Taylor, Shelley, et al., 'Bio-behavioral Responses to Stress in Females: Tend-and-Befriend, not Fight-or-Flight', *Psychological Review*, 2000

page 139 Physical movement: Siegel, Daniel, and Payne Bryson, Tina, *The Whole-Brain Child: 12 Revolutionary Strategies to Nurture Your Child's Developing Mind*, New York: Random House Publishing Group, 2011

page 146 Glitter jar: Willard, Christopher, *Growing Up Mindful: Essential Practices to Help Children, Teens, and Families Find Balance, Calm, and Resilience*, Louisville, CO: Sounds True, 2016

page 150 Wired for risk: Galván, Adriana, 'Why the brains of teenagers excel at taking risks', *Aeon*, 14 June 2016

page 150 Teenage brain: E.B., 'How teenage brains are different', *The Economist*, 18 March 2015

page 151 Disregard for consequences: Siegel, Daniel, *Brainstorm: The Power and Purpose of the Teenage Brain*, New York: Jeremy P. Tarcher/Penguin, 2013

page 151 Sensitivity to peer pressure: Blakemore, Sarah-Jayne, *The Mysterious Workings of the Adolescent Brain*, TEDGlobal, 2012

page 152 Interpretation of facial expression: van Beek, Yolanda, and Semon Dubas, Judith, 'Age and gender differences in decoding basic and non-basic facial expressions in late childhood and early adolescence', *Journal of Nonverbal Behavior*, 2008

—— Yurgelun-Todd, Deborah, 'Emotional and cognitive changes during adolescence', *Current Opinion in Neurobiology*, 2007

page 153 Out of sync: Foster, Russell, 'Why teenagers really do need an extra hour in bed', *New Scientist*, 17 April 2013

page 154 Teensleep project at University of Oxford: www.ndcn.ox.ac.uk/research/sleep-circadian-neuroscience-institute/research-projects-4/teensleep

Step 8

page 169 'Name it to tame it': Siegel, Daniel, and Payne Bryson, Tina, *The Whole-Brain Child: 12 Revolutionary Strategies to Nurture Your Child's Developing Mind*, New York: Random House Publishing Group, 2011

page 190 Sensitive children: Aron, Elaine, *The Highly Sensitive Child: Helping Our Children Thrive When the World Overwhelms Them*, New York: Harmony Books, 2002

page 192 'Orchid' and 'dandelion' children: Boyce, Thomas, and Ellis, Bruce, 'Biological Sensitivity to Context', *Development and Psychopathology*, 2005

Step 9

page 198 The term 'Digital Natives' was coined by the US writer and speaker on education Marc Prensky in 2001: Prensky, Marc, 'Digital Natives, Digital Immigrants', *On the Horizon*, Bradford: MCB University Press, 2001

page 205 BeatYourselfUpBook: Keegan, Natalie, 'Mumsnet user calls for mums not to compare themselves to others on "BeatYourselfUpBook"', *Sun*, 3 April 2016

Step 10

page 223 Research Center for Healthy Minds: Davidson, Richard, www.centerhealthyminds.org/about/overview

page 238 Brain-imaging study on meditation: Lutz, Antoine, et al., 'Long-term meditators self-induce high-amplitude gamma synchrony during mental practice', *Proceedings of the National Academy of Sciences*, 2004

page 239 Children's kindness project: Action for Happiness, 'Children's kindness project inspires commuters', www.actionforhappiness.org/news/childrens-kindness-project-inspires-commuters, 28 November 2014

page 239 Acts of kindness: Russell, Bernadette, *Do Nice, Be Kind, Spread Happy: Acts of Kindness for Kids (Random Acts of Kindness)*, Brighton: Ivy Press, 2014

page 240 Hooper, Ryan, and Heads, Laura, '"I wanted to cry": Young mum receives heartwarming letter from stranger on train', *Mirror*, 25 January 2015

page 240 Beattie, Kieran, 'Kind-hearted Aberdeen schoolboy, 7, donates birthday presents to local food bank', *Press and Journal*, 1 February 2016

page 240 Moran, Lee, 'Store worker's beautiful deed for blind girl with autism goes viral', *Huffington Post*, 8 May 2016

Resources

Mental health support organizations for adults

Mental Health Foundation

www.mentalhealth.org.uk

A mental health research, policy and service-improvement charity that aims to improve the lives of those with mental health problems or learning disabilities.

Mind

www.mind.org.uk

A charity providing mental health advice and support. Mind also campaigns to improve services, raise awareness and promote understanding.

No Panic

www.nopanic.org.uk

Helpline: 0844 967 4848

Voluntary charity offering support for sufferers of panic attacks and Obsessive Compulsive Disorder (OCD).

Relate: The Relationship People

www.relate.org.uk

Helpline: 0300 100 1234

Every year Relate helps more than a million people of all ages, backgrounds and sexual orientations to strengthen their relationships through its counselling services.

Samaritans

www.samaritans.org

Helpline: 116 123

Samaritans is available 24 hours a day to provide confidential emotional support to people experiencing feelings of distress, despair or suicidal thoughts.

Finding a therapist

Association for Family Therapy and Systemic Practice (AFT)

www.aft.org.uk

Britain's leading organization for family therapy and systemic psychotherapists. Its members work with children, young people and adults, couples, families and individuals.

British Association for Counselling and Psychotherapy (BACP)

www.bacp.co.uk

A professional body for counsellors and psychotherapists accredited by the Professional Standards Authority for Health and Social Care.

British Psychological Society (BPS)
www.bps.org.uk

The British Psychological Society is the representative body for psychology and psychologists in Britain, and is responsible for the development, promotion and application of psychology for the public good. Its directory of Chartered Psychologists can help you find a qualified therapist.

Counselling Directory
www.counselling-directory.org.uk

Counselling Directory has developed a service that brings together all the information needed to help connect people with the right counsellor or professional support for them.

Mindfulness

Be Mindful
www.bemindful.co.uk

Run by the Mental Health Foundation, this programme helps you to learn mindfulness online or find a teacher or course in your area. Courses are nationwide and are secular and science-based.

Mindful
www.mindful.org

A website with lots of information and practical tips from the team behind *Mindful* magazine.

UK Network for Mindfulness-Based Teacher Training Organizations
www.mindfulness-network.org/listingspagenew.php

A directory of mindfulness teachers who have demonstrated that they meet UK good practice guidelines. It includes lists of affiliated organizations and resources.

Meditation Centres

Gaia House
www.gaiahouse.co.uk

Gaia House is a meditation retreat centre offering silent meditation retreats in the Buddhist tradition.

London Insight Meditation
www.londoninsight.org

This small, independent charity promotes insight meditation, plus related practices, values and teachings from the Buddhist tradition.

Vipassana Meditation

www.dipa.dhamma.org

This organization offers ten-day residential silent retreats to learn Vipassana meditation. Courses are run on a donation-only basis.

Organizations for young people and parents

Action for Children

www.actionforchildren.org.uk

A charity committed to helping vulnerable and neglected children and young people.

Childline

www.childline.org.uk

Helpline: 0800 1111

Childline is a private and confidential service for children and young people up to the age of nineteen. Call their helpline, chat online, or send an email.

Family Lives

www.familylives.org.uk

Helpline: 0808 800 2222

A national family-support charity providing parenting help and support in all aspects of family life.

RESOURCES

MindEd
www.minded.org.uk

Parents who are concerned about their child's mental health and well-being can visit this excellent site to access good-quality information. MindEd also features advice from parents who support children with mental health problems.

Mindfulness in Schools Project (MiSP)
www.mindfulnessinschools.org

MiSP was established in 2009 as a not-for-profit organization. It aims to bring mindfulness to young people and those who care for them in order to advance their well-being and resilience.

National Children's Bureau
www.ncb.org.uk

A charitable organization dedicated to advancing the health and well-being of all children and young people across every aspect of their lives, and providing them with a powerful and authoritative voice.

NSPCC
www.nspcc.org.uk

Helpline: 0808 800 5000

A leading charity aiming to prevent child abuse and help children and families recover from its effects. If you're worried about a child – even if you're unsure – you can contact their professional counsellors 24 hours a day for help, advice and support.

Papyrus

www.papyrus-uk.org

Helpline: 0800 068 4141

A national charity dedicated to the prevention of young suicide, Papyrus runs a confidential helpline called HOPELineUK for young persons at risk of suicide and anybody who is worried about them.

Reading Well Books on Prescription

www.reading-well.org.uk

A source of recommendations for expert-endorsed books about mental health aimed at thirteen- to eighteen-year-olds. It covers topics including anxiety, stress and OCD, as well as bullying and exams. Books are available to borrow from public libraries.

YoungMinds

www.youngminds.org.uk

Helpline for parents: 0808 802 5544

A charity committed to improving the emotional well-being and mental health of children and young people.

Provides information for parents and professionals, runs training workshops, campaigns and conducts research.

Further reading and helpful organizations for specific issues

Anxiety and anger

Collins-Donnelly, Kate, *Starving the Anxiety Gremlin: A Cognitive Behavioural Therapy Workbook on Anxiety Management for Young People*, Gremlin and Thief CBT Workbook, London: Jessica Kingsley Publishers, 2013

Creswell, Cathy, and Willetts, Lucy, *Overcoming Your Child's Fears and Worries: A Self-help Guide Using Cognitive Behavioral Techniques*, London: Robinson, 2007

Huebner, Dawn, *What to Do When You Worry Too Much: A Kid's Guide to Overcoming Anxiety* (*What to Do Guides for Kids*), Washington, DC: Magination Press, 2005

Siegel, Daniel, and Payne Bryson, Tina, *The Whole-Brain Child: 12 Revolutionary Strategies to Nurture Your Child's Developing Mind*, New York: Random House Publishing Group, 2011

Whitehouse, Éliane, and Pudney, Warwick, *A Volcano in My Tummy: Helping Children to Handle Anger*, Gabriola, BC: New Society Publishers, 1998

Autism Spectrum Disorder (ASD)

National Autistic Society (NAS)
www.autism.org.uk

Helpline: 0808 800 4104

Provides information for parents and carers about autism and runs an online community and a confidential parent-to-parent telephone service.

Bereavement

Winston's Wish: The Charity for Bereaved Children
www.winstonswish.org.uk

Helpline: 08088 020 021

Support, guidance and information for anyone caring for a bereaved child or a child facing the imminent death of a family member.

Child Bereavement UK
www.childbereavementuk.org

Helpline: 0800 02 888 40

Supports families and educates professionals when a baby or child of any age dies or is dying, or when a child is facing bereavement.

Cruse Bereavement Care

www.cruse.org.uk

Helpline: 0808 808 1677

Promotes the well-being of bereaved people and aims to enable anyone who has been bereaved to understand their grief and cope with their loss.

Body image

Be Real Campaign

www.berealcampaign.co.uk

A national movement of individuals, schools, businesses, charities and public bodies campaigning to change attitudes to body image. It was launched in response to the 'Reflections on Body Image' report by the All-Party Parliamentary Group for Body Image.

Body Gossip

www.bodygossip.org

A charity promoting body confidence. It delivers an education programme to teenagers aged 13–18 in secondary schools all over Britain.

Bullying

Bullying UK (Part of Family Lives)

www.bullying.co.uk

Helpline: 0808 800 2222

Offers extensive practical advice and information about bullying for young people, and its website has a section on bullying at school.

Bullybusters

www.bullybusters.org.uk

Helpline: 0800 169 6928

Provides information on bullying and runs an anti-bullying initiative that offers training and awareness sessions for schools, professionals and parents.

Kidscape

www.kidscape.org.uk

Helpline for concerned family members: 0207 823 5430

A charity that equips young people, parents and professionals with the skills to tackle bullying and safeguarding issues across Britain.

RESOURCES

Digital technology and online safety

Hayman, Suzie, and Coleman, John, *Parents and Digital Technology: How to Raise the Connected Generation*, London: Routledge, 2016

Janis-Norton, Noel, *Calmer Easier Happier Screen Time: For Parents of Toddlers to Teens, a Guide to Getting Back in Charge of Technology*, London: Yellow Kite, 2016

Childnet
www.childnet.com

A non-profit organization working to help make the internet a great and safe place for children. Includes advice on making family contracts to manage use of the internet.

Cybersmile Foundation
www.cybersmile.org

A non-profit organization tackling all forms of online bullying and hate campaigns.

Internet Matters
www.internetmatters.org

A website that helps parents keep their children safe online. It includes age-specific practical tips and resources covering areas including: parental controls, managing cyberbullying, sexting, inappropriate content and online grooming.

NSPCC and O2

www.nspcc.org.uk and www.o2.co.uk/help/nspcc

Helpline: 0808 800 5002

Phone company O2 has joined forces with the NSPCC to help keep children safe online. Whether you want to set up parental controls, adjust privacy settings or get advice on social networks, you can call experts from O2 and NSPCC on their helpline seven days a week.

Thinkuknow

www.thinkuknow.co.uk

An education programme about sexual abuse underpinned by the latest intelligence from the National Crime Agency's Child Exploitation and Online Protection Centre command. Thinkuknow aims to ensure that children, young people, their parents and carers, and the professionals who work with them, all have access to timely and practical information.

UK Safer Internet Centre

www.saferinternet.org.uk

Helpline: 0344 381 4772

Provides e-safety tips, advice and resources to help children and young people stay safe online.

Drugs and alcohol

Talk to Frank

www.talktofrank.com

Helpline: 0300 123 6600

Confidential helpline and detailed information about drugs and alcohol for families.

Eating disorders

Bryant-Waugh, Rachel, *Eating Disorders: A Parents' Guide*, London: Routledge, 2004

Anorexia and Bulimia Care

www.anorexiabulimiacare.org.uk

Helpline: 03000 11 12 13

A national organization providing care, emotional support and practical guidance for anyone affected by eating disorders: sufferers, their families, carers and professionals.

Beat

www.b-eat.co.uk

Helpline: 0345 634 1414

A charity supporting people affected by eating disorders.

Gender issues

Gender Identity Development Service (GIDS)
www.gids.nhs.uk

Established in 1989, GIDS is a specialized clinic commissioned by NHS England for young people presenting with difficulties with their gender identity.

Obsessive Compulsive Disorder (OCD)

Derisley, Jo, *Breaking Free from OCD: A CBT Guide for Young People and Their Families*, London: Jessica Kingsley Publishers, 2008

OCD-UK
www.ocduk.org

Supporting children and adults affected by OCD.

Play, nature and resilience

Brown, Stuart, and Vaughan, Christopher, *Play: How It Shapes the Brain, Opens the Imagination, and Invigorates the Soul*, New York: Avery/Putnam, 2009

Ginsburg, Kenneth, *Building Resilience in Children and Teens: Giving Kids Roots and Wings*, Elk Grove Village, IL: American Academy of Pediatrics, 2011

Hanscom, Angela, *Balanced and Barefoot: How Unrestricted Outdoor Play Makes for Strong, Confident, and Capable Children*, Oakland, CA: New Harbinger, 2016

Louv, Richard, *Last Child in the Woods: Saving Our Children from Nature-Deficit Disorder*, London: Atlantic Books, 2010

Self-harm

Smith, Jane, *The Parent's Guide to Self Harm: What Parents Need to Know*, Oxford: Lion Books, 2012

National Self-Harm Network
www.nshn.co.uk

Helpline: 0800 622 6000

A national charity to provide support to people who self-harm, and those affected by self-harm, including family and professionals. They have useful resources that can be downloaded on understanding more about self-harm and strategies to encourage other ways of coping with difficult emotions.

Inspiring organizations for parents and children

Action for Happiness
www.actionforhappiness.org

Members take action in their homes, workplaces, schools and local communities to create a happier world, with fewer people suffering from mental health problems and more people feeling good, functioning well and helping others.

EarthCraftuk

www.earthcraftuk.com

A community interest company aiming to embed a 'Forest School' ethos into the educational framework in the south-east of England.

Embercombe

www.embercombe.org

A charity and social enterprise that runs experiential and leadership programmes for children, teenagers and adults. It aims to reconnect people to nature, community and themselves through transformative experiences.

LIFEbeat

www.lifebeat.co.uk

A charity providing transformational learning experiences for teenagers and adults through week-long summer camps for 14–18-year-olds, followed up with mentoring support and reunions. LIFEbeat's approach is based around the Creative Community Model originally created by Partners for Youth Empowerment in the US.

More on mindfulness

General:

Brach, Tara, *True Refuge: Finding Peace and Freedom in Your Own Awakened Heart*, London: Hay House, 2013

Chödrön, Pema, *When Things Fall Apart: Heart Advice for Difficult Times*, Shaftesbury, Dorset: Element Books, 2007

Heaversedge, Jonty, and Halliwell, Ed, *The Mindful Manifesto: How Doing Less and Noticing More Can Help Us Thrive In a Stressed-out World*, London: Hay House, 2012

Huber, Cheri, and Narayanan, Ashwini, *I Don't Want To, I Don't Feel Like It: How Resistance Controls Your Life and What to Do About It*, Murphys, CA: Keep It Simple Books, 2013

Kabat-Zinn, Jon, *Full Catastrophe Living: How To Cope With Stress, Pain and Illness Using Mindfulness Meditation*, London: Piatkus, 1996

Nhat Hanh, Thich, *The Miracle of Mindfulness: The Classic Guide to Meditation by the World's Most Revered Master*, London: Rider, 1991

Wax, Ruby, *A Mindfulness Guide for the Frazzled*, London: Penguin Life, 2016

Williams, Mark, and Penman, Danny, *Mindfulness: A Practical Guide to Finding Peace in a Frantic World*, London: Piatkus, 2011

Williams, Mark, et al., *The Mindful Way Through Depression: Freeing Yourself from Chronic Unhappiness*, New York: Guilford Press, 2007

Helping children to learn mindfulness:

Hawn, Goldie, and Holden, Wendy, *10 Mindful Minutes: Giving Our Children – and Ourselves – the Skills to Reduce Stress and Anxiety for Healthier, Happier Lives*, London: Piatkus, 2012

Kaiser Greenland, Susan, *The Mindful Child: How to Help Your Kid Manage Stress and Become Happier, Kinder and More Compassionate*, New York: Atria, 2010

Kerr, Christiane, *Bedtime Meditations for Kids (Calm Kids)*, Borough Green: Diviniti Publishing, 2005

Snel, Eline, *Sitting Still Like a Frog: Mindfulness Exercises for Kids (and Their Parents)*, Boulder, CO: Shambhala Publications, 2014

Personal growth, parenting and neuroscience

Brown, Brené, *Daring Greatly: How the Courage to Be Vulnerable Transforms the Way We Live, Love, Parent, and Lead*, New York: Gotham Books, 2012

Faber, Adele, and Mazlish, Elaine, *How to Talk So Teens Will Listen and Listen So Teens Will Talk*, London: Piccadilly Press, 2006

RESOURCES

Gilbert, Paul, *The Compassionate Mind (Compassion Focused Therapy)*, London: Constable, 2010

Hanson, Rick, *Buddha's Brain: The Practical Neuroscience of Happiness, Love and Wisdom*, Oakland, CA: New Harbinger, 2009

Hughes, Daniel, and Baylin, Jonathan, *Brain-Based Parenting: The Neuroscience of Caregiving for Healthy Attachment*, New York: W.W. Norton, 2012

Jensen, Frances, *The Teenage Brain: A Neuroscientist's Survival Guide to Raising Adolescents and Young Adults*, London: Harper Thorson, 2015

Kabat-Zinn, Jon, and Kabat-Zinn, Myla, *Everyday Blessings: The Inner Work of Mindful Parenting*, London: Hachette Books, 1998

Kornfield, Jack, *A Path with Heart: A Guide Through the Perils and Promises of Spiritual Life*, London: Bantam, 1993

Levine, Amir, and Heller, Rachel, *Attached: Identify Your Attachment Style and Find Your Perfect Match*, London: Penguin, 2010

Morgan, Nicola, *Blame My Brain: The Amazing Teenage Brain Revealed*, London: Walker Books, updated edn 2013

Neff, Kristin, *Self Compassion: Stop Beating Yourself Up and Leave Insecurity Behind*, London: Yellow Kite, 2011

Neufeld, Gordon, and Maté, Gabor, *Hold Onto Your Kids: Why Parents Need to Matter More Than Peers*, New York: Ballantine Books, 2006

Parkin, John, C., *F*** It: The Ultimate Spiritual Way*, London: Hay House, 2014

Perry, Bruce, and Szalavitz, Maia, *Born for Love: Why Empathy Is Essential – and Endangered*, New York: William Morrow, 2010

Richo, David, *When Love Meets Fear: Becoming Defense-less and Resource-full*, Mahwah, NJ: Paulist Press, 1997

Senior, Jennifer, *All Joy and No Fun: The Paradox of Modern Parenthood*, London: Virago, 2015

Siegel, Daniel, and Hartzell, Mary, *Parenting from the Inside Out: How a Deeper Self-understanding Can Help You Raise Children Who Thrive*, New York: Jeremy P. Tarcher/Penguin, 2003

Siegel, Daniel, *Brainstorm: The Power and Purpose of the Teenage Brain*, New York: Jeremy P. Tarcher/Penguin, 2013

Stiffelman, Susan, *Parenting with Presence: Practices for Raising Conscious, Confident, Caring Kids* (Eckhart Tolle edn), Novato, CA: New World Library, 2015

Tolle, Eckhart, *A New Earth: Create a Better Life*, New York: Dutton/Penguin, 2005

Tolle, Eckhart, *The Power of Now: A Guide to Spiritual Enlightenment*, London: Yellow Kite, 2001

Recommended apps

Headspace: Guided meditation and mindfulness

www.headspace.com

Among the best-known and most popular mindfulness apps, Headspace was co-founded by mindfulness expert Andy Puddicombe to make meditation more accessible. It includes guided meditations suitable for all levels as well as specific content focused on creativity, decreasing stress and increasing happiness.

Available on iTunes and Google Play.

Smiling Mind: Guided meditation and mindfulness (free)

www.smilingmind.com.au

Created in Australia by psychologists and educators, Smiling Mind was originally designed to help children and young people de-stress and stay calm. There are tailored programmes for different age groups starting at 7–11.

Available on iTunes and Google Play.

Calm: Guided meditations and relaxation (free)

www.calm.com

This simple-to-use app aims to help you meditate, sleep or relax. It includes the 'Seven Steps of Calm', which is aimed at beginners and experienced meditators alike, as well as other guided sessions running from 2–30 minutes with a range of background scenes and nature sounds.

Available on iTunes and Google Play.

Mindfulness Bell (free)
Set it to ring a Tibetan singing bowl at intervals throughout the day to remind you to take a pause and check in with yourself.

Available on Google Play.

Insight Timer (free)
www.insighttimer.com

A meditation timer that doubles as a mindfulness guide and includes guided meditations by well-known teachers such as Eckhart Tolle, Thich Nhat Hanh, Tara Brach, Jack Kornfield, Jon Kabat-Zinn and others.

Available on iTunes and Google Play.

Gratitude Journal – the original!
www.happytapper.com

A well-known gratitude journal founded by Carla White in 2008. You can add photos, tag Facebook friends, geotag your entries, and share what you're grateful for with loved ones.

Available on iTunes and Google Play.

Gratitude Garden (free)

www.izzymcrae.com/gratitude

This excellent, innovative app designed by Izzy McRae helps you maintain a gratitude practice by noting down three good things that have happened over the past 24 hours. As you progress, you receive points you can use to build a virtual 'garden'.

Available on iTunes and Google Play.

EasyPeasy

www.easypeasyapp.com

EasyPeasy supports learning through play at home, helping children develop the skills they need for school and beyond. Children develop key skills like concentration, creativity and determination through positive play and positive interactions with their parents.

Acknowledgements

This book is the fruit of all I have learned from the hundreds of families I've had the privilege of working with, and I would like to thank them for the trust they have placed in me during our sessions together and the many lessons they have taught me. Parents are building the foundations of all our tomorrows – and they are all heroes.

I owe everything in my life to my grandparents, Marguerite and Peter. The kindest, gentlest and most caring man I ever met, my granddad died at the age of eighty-eight, while I was working on this book. He and Nanny showed me all the love, patience and tenderness any child could have wished for. My granddad always encouraged me to follow my dreams and told me that anything was possible: and this book is proof he was right. I know my mum Amanda's influence has also flowed through these pages – and that she is still watching my progress from beyond the veil of everyday reality. I'd also like to thank the rest of my family, including Auntie Vivien, Paul, my cousin Josh, my cousin Alex and his wife Laura, and my Auntie June for all the love and support they provided while this book was being written.

ACKNOWLEDGEMENTS

I'd also like to thank those who showed me so much kindness when I was going through my own difficult times in childhood, including Julie and John Gilham, Rachael Fleming, Mary, John and Rebecca Wright and my godparents Graham and Margaret. I also owe a great debt to Charlotte Corbett, Margaret Norden, and all at the Central School of Dancing in Norwich.

A very special thank you to my wonderful partner, Matt, who has been there for me on this writing journey every step of the way, and who has turned every day into an adventure in love and laughter.

My friends have been an ever-ready source of insight, humour and encouragement, especially Kirsty Young, Katie Rogers, Katie Coldham, and Annette Sloly and her husband David. Many thanks also to Rose Latham, Sarah Chandler, Julie Damant, Catriona Metcalfe, Louise Taylor, Emma Sisley, Hannah Nedas, Nicola Gambin, Jane Bradbury, Ramona Burrage and Edward Walsh. Daniel Simpson, Katie Green, Justin Quirk and Kate Holt have also been unflagging and inspiring supporters of this project.

At the University of Kent, I'd like to thank Professors Derek Rutter and Lyn Quine, who supervised my masters in health psychology. I would not have been able to complete this course without the generous support of the Royal Pinner School Foundation, to whom I am eternally indebted. I am also extremely grateful for the incredible opportunity I had to train at Salomons, Canterbury Christ Church University, and to all the expert tutors and supervisors who taught me so much about psychology, and myself. A special thanks to Professor Paul Camic and Dr Louise Goodbody.

In more recent times, I've had the privilege of working with, and learning from, my many fantastic colleagues in the NHS, in private practice and in the public sector, who are too numerous to name but whose wisdom and skill has informed every one of these pages.

As a newcomer to publishing, I could not have asked for a more supportive and visionary team than my agent Claire Conrad of Janklow & Nesbit, my publisher Brenda Kimber and all at Transworld, and my television agent Jo Wander at Wander Management. Thank you for your patient guidance and the faith you have had in *Happy Parent, Happy Child*.

Index

INDEX

INDEX

INDEX

INDEX

INDEX

INDEX

About the author

Dr Genevieve von Lob is a clinical psychologist who has worked with families from every type of background during a ten-year career spanning private practice, NHS Child and Adolescent Mental Health Services and work for local authorities. She has been widely quoted in the media, including in the *Telegraph*, *Financial Times*, *Top Santé* and *Gràzia*, and featured as a consultant therapist in an episode of Channel 4's *Dispatches*. She lives in south-west London and enjoys playing the piano and singing in her spare time.

www.drvonlob.com